# Retirement
# Planning
# Beyond 55

## Dr. Paul O'Neill, Ed. D., CFP®

# Acknowledgements

Many thanks to Erin and Jim Doppke for their greatly appreciated assistance in formatting and editing this book; to Scott Schatzle, CFP® and Carol Chollar for their thorough review of the manuscript; and to my wife Kathie for her constant encouragement throughout the writing process.

# Table of Contents

# Introduction

## Who should read this book?

A person could fill a small library with all the books related to financial and retirement planning. You may have read several of these books. If so, you're likely wondering whether this book will be of help to you.

As the title suggests, this book was written for a fairly selective audience: **those beyond age 55 who feel a need to review and improve their retirement financial plans**. All of the strategies, specific techniques, and examples in this book focus on the needs of those in this critical phase of retirement planning.

What about those younger than 55? Many sections of this book will address their needs, because it contains fundamentally sound financial ideas and techniques applicable to all ages. That said, this book will be of the greatest value to those people who are approaching, or who have begun, retirement from their primary income-producing job.

## Why should you use me as your guide?

My role in this book is to be your guide through the sometimes confusing world of personal retirement finances. As such, it is only fair for me to give you my qualifications for this role.

To begin with, I am a CERTIFIED FINANCIAL PLANNER™ professional. The CFP® mark is the most recognized certification in the world of personal financial planning, one that I earned following a career teaching financial markets and strategic planning in an MBA program. I also have a doctorate in adult continuing education, so I know something about the best way to help you continue learning about the world of personal financial planning.

I have also had considerable experience in helping people improve their financial plans. This includes my work as the founder and principal of O'Neill Financial Planning LLC (ONeillFinancialPlanning.com), based in Estero, Florida. Through my firm, I am a registered investment adviser with the state of Florida.

In addition to my state registration, academic and professional credentials, and financial planning experience, I have been making the same journey that all of you are now taking. I have had to personally work through many of the same issues that you are dealing with. In doing so, I have used all of the key strategies and techniques in this book. My goal is to make it easy for you to use these tools in improving your own personal retirement financial plan.

## Why might you *really* need this book?

Simply put, many individuals clearly need help with their investments and their retirement plans. For example, the market researcher Dalbar reports most individual stock investors have recently had an average annual return of 3.5%, compared to the S&P 500's annualized return of 7.8%. In the same vein, some mutual funds report that individual (as opposed to institutional) accounts get as little as 50% of the total return of their fund. The main cause of these dismal individual investor results: poor market timing in buying and selling stocks. This is because individuals unfortunately tend to do a lot of panic selling (from fear), when the market is near a low point; and they do a lot of bandwagon buying (from greed), when the market is near a high point.

It's hard to blame individuals that became fearful in the Great Recession as their stock investments dropped 60%; it's also hard to blame individuals for becoming greedy when the stock market later went up 100%. How can we keep these emotions under control in challenging financial times? In short, we need a new set of strategies.

In the chapters to follow, I will discuss strategies that will result in us taking a much more businesslike, objective, and rational approach toward handling our finances. Many of these strategies have been drawn from those I developed for my MBA financial and planning courses. Others have been developed from my work during and after my CFP® certification process. The application of these business strategies represents what I believe to be a unique and valuable contribution to the world of retirement planning.

## How can you best use this book?

The first part of the book deals with the most common and immediate financial concerns. It should be helpful to you as you address whether you are on the right retirement financial track right now - and if not, what you can do about it.

The second part takes you through the complete planning process – from establishing goals through to the development of a comprehensive plan – using tools and ideas adapted from MBA courses. This section will be especially useful for those who have never established a formal financial plan, or for those who would like to make a strategic review of their finances.

The third part presents some detailed examples and further exploration of the topics discussed in earlier chapters.

The fourth part includes an appendix of brief definitions or explanations of terms used in the book, such as "401(k)" or "403(b)" accounts, or a "share" of a publicly traded company. It also features a guide to the financial courses at Khan Academy, and a listing of the best ways to search for a CFP® professional.

One cautionary note: This book is not intended to be a comprehensive repository of all possible ideas for improving your retirement plans. However, it does contain what I believe to be the best current and pragmatic financial planning ideas, including ones that I have personally used for clients.

My sincere hope is that by reading this book, you will be able to take more effective control over your retirement planning. This can be accomplished by either learning how to use these strategies and techniques totally on your own, or by being better able to work with a professional advisor, such as a CFP® professional.

# PART 1

Immediate Financial Concerns

# Chapter 1: Will I be financially secure in retirement?

> Retirement is like a long vacation in Las Vegas. The goal is to enjoy it to the fullest, but not so fully that you run out of money.
>
> – Jonathan Clements

This chapter will help you answer a basic question: How do I make sure that I have sufficient financial resources for my retirement – which, for planning purposes, is normally a 30-year span?

There are really three parts to this broad question, to be discussed in the first four chapters:

1) Do I have enough overall money to cover my entire retirement? (this chapter)
2) How can I provide a secure funding for my basic living expenses? (Chapter 2)
3) After meeting my basic living expenses, how can I get a sufficient return on my investments so I can achieve all the other important goals in my retirement? (Chapter 3 and 4)

We begin with the first question: Overall how much do I need?

Here's a simplistic answer: You need enough so that your cash inflow matches your cash outflow throughout your retirement! However, as always, the devil will be in the details – how exactly can you do this?

## A quick way to figure our expected spending

When it comes to spending, our past and current behavior can be a good predictor of our future behavior. Thus, in order to know how much spending to plan for, you will first review your past spending. A simple way to start is to review your last 12 bank statements. On each you will see a line that adds up the total withdrawals for that month. Add these up and you will get the total amount you spent from your checking account for one year. This should represent 85-90% of your total spending, but we don't have the full picture yet.

To get the full picture, you'll make a series of adjustments:

1) You probably had some additional payments, such as those with cash, or those deducted from your paycheck or from social security (like health insurance). You will add these to the total from your checking account.

2) Next you will have to adjust for unusual major expenditures. For example, if you took a vacation to Hawaii in which you spent $4000 more than your usual vacation, you should subtract the $4000.

3) On the other hand, if you didn't have to spend any money for home maintenance or for replacing appliances, and you usually spend $3000 for that, then you would add $3000 to your total expected spending. In a similar way, you should include money to eventually replace major items, like a car or furnace. This money will provide a reserve fund to cover expenditures like that without having to liquidate investments at a market low point.

4) Finally, you should consider any major adjustments that will occur in your retirement years. Will your healthcare insurance and payments go up? (Many people find that these go up significantly). Will you pay off a mortgage in 5 years? Will you be giving up an expensive hobby in 10 years? Will you purchase a condo or a time-share in 3 years? You will need to calculate the effect of these issues over your expected retirement years. (See Part 3 for a discussion of the pros and cons of holding a house mortgage in retirement.)

After finishing the adjustments, you will know exactly how much you are spending now, and you should have a good idea of your expected future annual spending.

## Now, let's look at our projected income

For this initial analysis, we will assume you are invested in a reasonably balanced, diversified investment portfolio of cash, bonds, and at least 50% stocks. (We'll discuss the details of this portfolio in Chapter 4, and later will consider the impact of having a much smaller portion of stocks.)

Let's begin the analysis by adding up your current or expected social security, pension, and annuity-type payments. Next, combine your IRA, 401(k), and personal investment accounts, and multiply by 4% (to calculate a safe withdrawal rate). Add this to the previous sum. This total sum, with an annual inflation adjustment, is a good ballpark measure of what you should be able to comfortably spend each year over a 30-year retirement.

Now, compare the spending and income numbers. If your projected income will match or exceed your anticipated spending, you are in great shape! You can now move on to the second chapter.

But what if your income number is short of your spending number? Not to worry! You have a number of options:

1) You may be able to delay your retirement payouts by choosing to work longer. For example, if you can work two more years, you can safely increase your investment withdrawal rate to 4.5%. The extra years of working can also delay your receipt of social security retirement benefits for two years, so the amount of the monthly payment you later receive will jump by 16%.

2) You can forego the annual inflation boost to your withdrawal amount in the years when you have negative investment returns. This would allow you to take out an additional 1/2% per year from your investments.

3) You can try to boost your investment return by taking on greater risk in the allocation of your investments – such as by going with 80% equity. I would <u>not</u> recommend this strategy for most people, as it would not be worth the sleepless nights when the market has a big slump.

4) You could increase your income by taking on a part-time job or other income-generating activity, like selling items on eBay.

5) You could adjust your spending by drawing up, and acting upon, a detailed budget plan. This will help you find ways to save money, and to better allocate money to the activities that are most important to you.

6) Some combination of the above.

Let's look at each of these options in some detail.

## Delaying retirement payouts

A great way to improve your projected retirement income is to continue to work for a while longer. There is a double advantage that creates the power of this strategy: You'll be able to grow your investments while decreasing the number of years needed for payouts.

In this option, you will add to your retirement investments, building on the normal return from these investments. As a result, for **each year** that you continue to work, you can raise your retirement withdrawal by approximately 1/4%.

Continuing to work will give you a better opportunity to delay social security payments, and thus be able to enjoy an increase of 8% for each delayed year (up to age 70).

Some may not have the physical ability or desire to continue their full-time work. Those in that position might consider "downsizing" their work – reducing their hours gradually as they prepare for retirement. One of my former colleagues found that gradually reducing his overall workload was a great way to transition from full-time work, to semi-retirement, to full retirement. At 66, he gave up a teaching position at the university, but he retained his consulting business. At 68, he gave up the management of that business, but he continued to consult. Now, at 70, he is ready for full retirement. By following this strategy, he was able to delay social security and receive higher benefits. He was also able to lower his initial withdrawals from his investment accounts. As a result, he is now able to retire with a significant boost to his retirement income.

Beyond the financial benefits, this type of transition provides the psychological benefits of gradually leaving your past work, while providing you the time to ease into new roles and activities. If you are able to follow this path, I strongly encourage you to take it.

### Foregoing the annual inflation boost to your withdrawal

One simple method to increase your initial withdrawal is to skip your annual inflation increase in "down" investment years. Most years you will be able to give yourself a raise to match the level of increase in inflation. But in those years when you get negative investment returns, you don't increase your withdrawal. Instead, you make small adjustments to lower your spending plans, especially in those categories most affected by inflation. As a result, you will not excessively reduce your core investments, the ones you will be counting on for future withdrawals. By following this option, you will be able to take out an additional ½% annual withdrawal.

## Taking on greater risk in the allocation of your investments

Over the long term, equities beat the return of fixed-income investments. The financial market compensates for the much greater volatility of equities by giving them a higher return. All other things equal, people would prefer a regular, steady return rather than one that might go down or up by 30%. So in order to attract investors, equities must offer a greater return over the long haul. For this reason, young investors are encouraged to have a high percentage of their investments in equities. They have the time to ride out market volatility, and benefit from higher total returns until retirement nears.

This picture changes when you get close to retirement. You need to retain more of the core value of your investments, so that you can easily handle the regular withdrawals that will support a lengthy retirement. And you don't have the luxury of the required time needed to rebuild from a big market dip; you might even be tempted to sell off your equities at the worst possible time. For these reasons, most retired people simply cannot afford the risk associated with an allocation of 80-100% equities.

> A frightened investor with 100% in equities goes to her broker and says she's worried about the volatility of the markets these days. The broker asks her how she has been sleeping. The investor says: She sleeps like a baby.
>
> The broker was amazed! "Really? Even with all the fluctuations in the market?"
>
> "Yup! I sleep for a couple of hours, and then I wake up and I cry for a couple of hours."

There may be some circumstances in which you could have a high portion of equities, and thus benefit from a higher overall investment return. Perhaps your social security, pension, and annuity income covers all of your basic living expenses, and most of your discretionary expenses. Or perhaps your living arrangements allow you to easily make a significant reduction in expenses, and you are willing to make that reduction if necessary. In these cases, you might consider raising your equity allocation and your annual withdrawal rate. You would, however, also need to be willing to live with what can be sleep-reducing shifts in the financial market. Again, most people don't want to go down this road.

## Increase your income through a part-time job or activity

You can consider taking on a "retirement job", something different from your previous full-time work.  This can be beneficial in ways beyond merely adding to your income. You might find yourself with more time on your hands than activities to fill the time. Or even if you have plenty to do, you might enjoy a break from retirement activities like home improvement projects, watching TV, or reading. In these cases, even a low-stress part-time job like working as a car jockey at an auto dealership or as a greeter at Wal-Mart might be an attractive option for some. For those that had a high-stress full time job, such work might not even feel like a real job. And you might even improve your relationship with others, as I heard one retiree remark: "Sometimes my wife just likes me to get out of the house!"

You might wish to take on a more challenging job, such as teaching at a local community college. This would generally require more time preparing to handle the work - for example, you would have to build up your teaching skills. But you might find it intellectually stimulating and intrinsically rewarding.

Another increasingly attractive option is to set up your own business. You could set up a consultancy, or you could sell items on eBay or Amazon (which could also help you get rid of unneeded items from your attic or garage). Keep in mind that self-employed people can now deduct all their healthcare insurance (including Medicare and Medicare supplement insurance) from their income, thus greatly reducing the net taxes on a part-time, small business.

## Adjust your spending by developing and using a written budget plan

Virtually everyone has some sort of budget for their spending, even if it is just in their head (when we find ourselves saying "I don't think we can afford that..."). However, if you are unable to close a financial gap on the income side, you will need to come up with a better budget plan to adjust your spending.

This better budget plan begins by tracking your expenses for three months. You'll want to determine how much you are currently spending for expense categories in both basic living expenses (such as food, shelter, and medical) and discretionary expenses (like cable TV, landscaping, and vacations).

Then you can evaluate and adjust these expenditures in light of your income and your goals. You can then use this budget to better guide your future spending. For more detailed guidance on the budgeting process, please see Part 3 of this book.

## Some combination of the above

To more easily achieve the balance between income and spending, you may want to use a combination of these options.

For example, if you are not retired, you may wish to extend your job in some form, while also delaying payouts from social security. Or if you are already retired, you might consider skipping the annual withdrawal inflation increase and developing a better budget plan.

To facilitate your decision-making, I strongly encourage you to use a spreadsheet that will help manipulate all these variables, such that you come up with the optimal plan for being financially comfortable throughout your retirement.

## Chapter summary

This chapter gave you the tools to construct a big picture, or 40,000-foot view, of your retirement financial status. You can quickly determine where you stand right now, and you can periodically re-assess to determine if you are moving in the right direction.

If you are not comfortable with your current financial status, you can begin to make the needed improvements by following the suggestions in this chapter. These options include ideas that affect both the income generating and the spending sides of our finances. These suggestions will be further explored in the succeeding chapters.

# Chapter 2: Improving your continuing, guaranteed cash flow

*How you <u>don't</u> want to define your CASH FLOW: The movement your money makes as it disappears down the drain.*

This chapter will address our second question dealing with a comfortable retirement - Do you have a secure funding for your basic living expenses?

Even if your projected retirement income matches up with projected spending, you should ensure that between 75-100% of your basic living expenses are covered by a guaranteed source of cash flow (such as pensions, social security, and annuities). While keeping in mind that nothing is fully guaranteed in life except death and taxes, you need to be confident that you will always have enough money to sufficiently cover these essential expenses.

This cash flow becomes your retirement paycheck. There are a couple of important reasons to ensure you have enough in this paycheck: You don't want to be worried at all about meeting these needs, and, without having the funding for basic living expenses, you may make poor decisions with your investment portfolio.

So, what do I mean by "basic living expenses"? These will vary somewhat from person to person. In general, basic living expenses include what you would think: food, shelter, clothes, medical care, transportation, taxes, and the like. These would usually represent 50-70% of your overall expenses.

Why do we think in terms of a <u>range</u> between 75-100% coverage of basic living expenses by guaranteed cash flow? If you want absolutely no financial risk (created by a fluctuation in returns) in the funding of these expenses, you should seek to have 100% coverage; if you are okay with some risk (some variation in exchange for a higher investment return), or if you have a large investment portfolio, you might wish to be closer to the 75%.

If your basic living expenses are sufficiently covered by a continuing, guaranteed cash flow, you can move on to Chapter 3. If not, read on!

So how can you increase your continuing cash flow paycheck? Let's look at each of the sources of essentially guaranteed cash flow for ways you might be able to get this increase.

## Traditional pensions

Traditional pensions pay out a fixed monthly amount (usually with cost of living adjustments) to retirees. Pension funds have been designed to invest money so that they will have cash for immediate disbursement, fixed-income for the intermediate timeframes, and conservative growth investments for the long term. Fully-funded pensions are those that actuaries have determined to be capable of meeting all their future payment obligations.

If you wish to increase your payments from a traditional pension, you will simply have to work longer in the job covered by the pension.

## Social security

By their nature, social security retirement benefits are intended to provide inflation-adjusted income throughout the life of the retiree. Some people question if social security payments will continue, at least at the promised level of benefits. In my opinion, if you are over 55, you can reasonably count on your social security retirement payments for the rest of your life, because:

1) There is a number of years of benefits guaranteed by the surplus in the social security trust fund (currently 18 years). This surplus is invested in US treasury bonds. While some point out correctly that this surplus fund is essentially composed of IOUs for excess social security tax receipts, the IOUs are indeed US government securities that are virtually risk-free.

2) Based on failed attempts to slightly cut the rate of increase in the cost of living adjustment to social security payments, it is hard to believe that Congress will allow the basic retirement payments to be lowered. It is much more likely Congress will take needed funds from general revenue, or, unfortunately, simply borrow more money. This latter action would be a continuation of what is actually going on right now, as the government is issuing more debt to replace the "surplus" IOUs as they are redeemed to pay current retirees. (Side note: There is clearly an increasing problem with the overall level of government debt, coupled with rising unfunded benefit promises in many government programs. However, I believe that social security retirement benefits will get the highest priority among government programs, and therefore the payments to those beyond 55 will be essentially guaranteed for at least the next 30 years.)

There are several ways to improve your payout from social security. Perhaps the simplest and most effective way is to delay when you start receiving retirement benefits. For each year you delay, up to age 70, you will receive an 8% larger monthly payment. If you are survived by a spouse, he or she will be eligible to receive a survivor benefit equivalent to your larger payment. This can be especially beneficial if your spouse is younger than you. And if you have an extra-long life, the added benefits provide a type of "longevity insurance" that can help cover expenses when your investments may have diminished. See Part 3 for more discussion of the advantages of waiting to receive social security benefits.

Spouses are able to receive the higher of two benefit amounts: one, based on their own work record, or two, based on 50% of their spouses' benefit at their full retirement age. The spousal benefit also applies to divorced couples who have been married for at least 10 years. For example, an ex-wife who didn't remarry can claim a benefit on her former husband's record, and get 35% of his benefit at 62, or 50% at her full retirement age.

For more information, specific to your own situation, I would strongly suggest that you further research this topic, then have follow-up discussions with people such as a social security representative and a financial advisor.

## Railroad retirement

Those who have worked over 10 years for railroads are eligible to receive Railroad Retirement. It is comprised of "Tier I", which is essentially social security, plus "Tier II", which is an additional railroad pension.

If you worked all your life for railroads, you have little incentive to delay receiving your benefits beyond age 65. While doing so would provide a larger Tier I benefit, you will receive no larger Tier II benefit. Thus, for most people in this situation, it would simply not make much sense to delay receiving benefits beyond 65.

However, if you have split your working life between railroad and non-railroad employers, you have a wonderful benefit of which few are aware. You can receive your Railroad Retirement payments at 65 or 66, and have all of your non-railroad employment social security credits count toward your Tier I benefit calculation. Then at age 70, you can apply for social security benefits based on both railroad and non-railroad earnings, and get delayed social security credits added to your benefits! This is great example as to why future retirees need to carefully investigate all "what if" questions well before they make their final decisions on social security and related pensions.

## Immediate annuities

If you make a lump sum payment to an insurance company, it can immediately provide you with a monthly fixed-payment annuity for the rest of your life. The annuity can be structured in various ways: to provide inflation increases; to additionally cover the life of your spouse; or to provide a minimum total benefit that would be paid to you and your survivors.

To get a better rate of return from your annuity, you could consider eliminating the minimum guaranteed payment to heirs, the inflation adjustment, and/or the spousal coverage. You could also wait for interest rates to rise, which will increase the initial annuity payment.

Please note: Not all annuities are immediate annuities. Most are called *variable annuities* because their returns vary with the stock market. They are thus not a source of guaranteed, continuing cash flow, and are consequently not recommended in this book for most investors.

If you are 65 or under, you may wish to consider a deferred fixed annuity, essentially an "immediate" annuity that will begin at a fixed time in the future.

For more information on immediate and deferred fixed annuities, see Part 3.

## TIAA-CREF annuities

This is a retirement plan option in a 403(b) plan for educators. These annuities have a guaranteed minimum contracted rate of return, adjusted upward as market conditions warrant. Payments are made over a lifetime or a minimum 10-year period.

A key way to increase your cash flow is to minimize the length of time for the payout. A payout schedule over a specified time (10 or 15 years) will yield a greater cash flow for that time, as compared to a lifetime payout.

## Guaranteed investment contracts

Guaranteed investment contracts are set up by insurance companies, and are most often found in 401(k) plans. Their return is based on short-to-medium fixed-income securities, and the interest rate is guaranteed for a year at a specified level.  Unlike with annuities, money can be withdrawn at any time.

If you convert a 401(k) to an IRA, you may be able to find better and higher paying guaranteed income options than these investment contracts.

## Chapter summary

For our peace of mind, it is important that we have an essentially guaranteed cash flow that will substantially cover our basic living expenses. If this cash flow is currently inadequate, we must fix it before we can determine the best choices for our investment money. This chapter gave us several ways to improve our guaranteed cash flow, including using an immediate annuity to bolster our retirement "paycheck".

Our next chapters will consider the best ways to use stocks and bonds to build our investment portfolio.

# Chapter 3: Do I really need to have stocks?

STOCK BULL MARKET - A random market movement causing an investor to mistake himself for a financial genius.

After assuring our basic needs are sufficiently covered by an essentially guaranteed cash flow, we turn our attention to how we should handle our investment money.

A key issue we must face: What role do we want common stocks to play in our investment portfolio?

## Stocks can be scary

Many retirees are afraid of stocks, and with good reason. As my retired dad once said to me: "Paul, I can't have a lot in stocks because I haven't got the time you have to make up for a big stock loss".

Let's spell out the risks of owning equity shares. Company stocks can:

- Become worthless, as happened with Enron and General Motors
- Experience great fluctuation in value
- Eliminate their dividends, as large banks did in the last financial crisis

If we are to use stocks in our investment plan, we must address these legitimate concerns. But before we do that, it would be helpful to remind ourselves of what stocks represent, and why their returns can be so substantial.

## Stocks can generate great wealth

Common stocks give us a share of business ownership in our economic system. And business ownership can provide a means of building great wealth, as a well-run business can generate profits far in excess of what an individual might earn from one's own individual labor. Realistically, not all of us can start up and run our own businesses, but all of us can participate in business by owning shares of publicly-traded companies.

Stocks collectively have doubled or tripled the investment return of fixed-income securities. Logically, this makes sense, because an equity security allows the owner to participate in the growing net income of the business, whereas the fixed-income security payment is limited to its interest rate. Further, stock owners know that there is greater risk associated with stocks, and thus will effectively demand a greater return before they make that investment.

## Are we playing with fire when we own stocks?

Because of the risk factors listed earlier, many people feel that one is playing with fire when owning stocks. Stocks can indeed be extremely risky – if you own them in the wrong way. If you own them in the right way, you can control their risks and derive great benefits from them.

Perhaps an analogy would be helpful. We all know that fire can be extremely dangerous – we frequently hear of people dying in house fires, especially in winter. However, we still use fire to heat our homes and cook our food. We have found ways to control the effect of fire such that we receive the benefits and yet greatly minimize the risk. Let's now discuss how we can control the risks from owning stocks.

## Controlling the risks associated with stocks

Let's look at each of the specific stock risks, and what can be done to minimize that risk.

### Complete failure of the company

It is quite unusual for a publicly-held company to completely go out of business – but of course, it can happen. However, there are several ways to control this risk:

- Be a careful purchaser of individual stocks. Make sure your choices are based on solid recommendations of experts, or do your own analysis.
- Monitor the status of the company. Keep up with the business and financial news about the company, and consider selling the stock if there has been a significant change since you purchased it.
- Have a diversified group of individual stocks. If a specific economic condition (e.g., low oil prices) depresses one company (e.g., an oil services company), it usually elevates other companies (e.g., a travel service company).

## Severe fluctuation in market value

Sometimes all stocks drop in value due to a general economic disruption. And occasionally these drops can become severe, as happened during the Great Recession that began in 2008. Here is how you can control the effects of this fluctuation:

- Diversify your stock holdings with fixed-income securities, especially bonds and treasuries. When economic conditions cause stocks to go down in value, fixed-income securities almost always go up in value. Having both types of securities in your investment portfolio limits the damage to the total value of your portfolio.
- Remember to be patient with the market. Fluctuations of 10% happen most years; fluctuations of 20% typically occur every 2-3 years. But the market always recovers from every downturn. Keeping this historical perspective will help you control your fears about market fluctuations.
- If you have a diversified portfolio of stocks and bonds, and there is an extended economic downturn, you might even consider selling some of your bonds, which now have inflated values, and then buy some stocks with artificially lowered values. When economic conditions improve, you then reverse this process: Sell these now more-highly valued stocks, and buy back some of the now-cheaper bonds. This is often referred to as "rebalancing your portfolio". If you are able to pull this off, you will have converted the downturn from a risk to an opportunity by improving the value of your portfolio. You will have followed the most important rule in investing: Buy low, sell high!

## Loss of dividends

In an economic downturn, it is common for companies in certain industries to reduce or even suspend their quarterly dividends. This happened during the Great Recession with many of the large banks. Here are some ways to deal with this concern:

- Diversify your stocks across many industries.
- Consider buying "dividend aristocrat" companies, ones that have a long history of maintaining and growing their dividends.
- Recognize that economic slumps do end, and market-wide dividend reductions are normally reversed within 2-3 years.

## A new game plan for stocks

In order to get the benefits of stocks, yet control the risks associated with them, we need a new game plan. This new strategy will:

- Help us control our emotions, especially the fear that causes people to make poor investing decisions.
- Help us recognize that stock market losses are only potential losses until they are realized by selling the stock. So if the market for the stock has a 10% decline, you really have not lost anything until you actually sell it.
- Allow us, not the markets, to be in charge - we can control when to sell the stock. This will inevitably improve our results. Imagine a baseball team that, during the season, is allowed to eliminate one preceding losing two-week period. The overwhelming odds are that the team would have a better overall record by exercising that option. We can accomplish the same sort of results by choosing not to sell a security while it is temporarily down in value.

This new plan is to use fixed-income securities to create a financial buffer between you and the stock market, allowing you to manage the timing of selling. Going back to our fire analogy: Instead of cooking with an open flame, we use a gas oven – benefiting from the fire without exposing ourselves directly to the fire.

The next chapter will outline the specific steps to implement this new game plan for investing with stocks.

## Chapter summary

Common stocks have an essential role to play in our investment portfolios. By using stocks in our investment portfolio, we can share in the earnings and growth of the business world.

However, we do need to find a way to minimize the inherent risks of stocks. We will discuss such a method in the next chapter.

# Chapter 4: The 3-Bucket plan

*"I have enough money to last me the rest of my life, unless I buy something."*

*– Jackie Mason*

Now on to our final question concerning a comfortable retirement - after I have met my basic needs, how can I make sure the return on my investments will finance all my other important goals for my retirement?

## Investment money is not for immediate basic expenses

I'll begin this chapter with a personal story.

I was discussing some financial planning ideas with a friend, when he turned to me and said: "Paul, I understand the need to have stocks in my investment portfolio. I know that over time they should give you a good return. But when the stock market goes down, and then my total investment value goes down, I get nervous. How do I deal with that?"

This incident reminded me of an important point: Handling investment money is different from handling living expense money – and we need to understand this difference if we are going to be really successful with our investments.

So let's take a fresh look at how we approach money in most circumstances, why that doesn't work for investments, and then look at how to develop a more effective strategy in investing that will reduce our concerns about market fluctuations.

## The one bucket view

Most of us tend to see all of our financial resources as being in one large bucket, into which we put our income, and out from which we take our spending. We can fairly easily track the level in this bucket; internet sites like Fidelity and Morgan Stanley can give us a daily total sum of all of our investments and bank accounts. If this overall number is going up or at least stable, we feel pretty good; if the number is dropping, we may feel we are in trouble and need to do something about it.

This thinking works pretty well for our pre-retirement income and spending. We put our paychecks into the bank, we write checks for spending, and we can see how we're doing by the balance in the checkbook. This approach can also be OK in retirement if our income is essentially from social security and pensions.

The problem comes when we see retirement money (including IRAs and 401(k)s) as being in the same bucket with the funds that are needed for immediate spending needs. In this mindset, when the inevitable, periodic declines hit the financial markets, the amount in the bucket drops, and a person nearing retirement may worry that she will not have enough in the bucket to cover future expenses. At a minimum, the individual frets that perhaps she should "take some investment money off the table". In the worst case, she may panic, and sell off all her equities to stop the drop in the bucket level. This is a terrible outcome for two reasons:

1) Virtually everyone facing a 30-year retirement will need to have at least some equities in a retirement investment portfolio. (Many financial experts recommend a 50-60% stock allocation throughout most of retirement.) By eliminating equities, the investor will likely incur a huge drop in projected total investment returns.
2) By selling when the market has dropped, the investor has locked in that loss, and will never have the opportunity to recover when the market shifts back in a positive direction.

## Creating three buckets

In order to avoid the panic described above, and yet ensure that we get a good return with a sufficient degree of security, we need to change our mindset. Instead of having one financial "bucket", we should create three, as discussed below.

### The Cash Bucket

This familiar bucket will hold our continuing cash flow from social security, pensions, annuities, and any work income. We'll draw from this bucket to pay all our expenses.

Since we need instant access to this money, and need to make sure it is safe, we most typically put the money from this bucket into a bank checking account. This provides us with a liquid, reliable, and traceable means of handling our transactions.

As discussed above, future retirees are highly concerned about maintaining the Cash Bucket. In an ideal world, retirees would simply convert all of their personal investment accounts into cash (or cash-like securities), and then use this pile of cash, along with social security and pension money, to cover bills. Realistically, few retirees are able to do this. Instead, almost everyone has to put most of their money to work in other financial securities, and then regularly have some of the securities converted into the cash needed to replenish the Cash Bucket. We'll be discussing how that works below.

How much should be in the Cash Bucket? Enough to make sure you cover at least one year of anticipated spending, plus have sufficient reserves for future "big ticket" purchases. So, for example, if you have $1.25 million in investments, you anticipate spending $100,000 in the next year, and will have $50,000 annual continuing cash flow from social security, a pension, and an annuity, you should have an average balance of $50,000 in your Cash Bucket. The rest of your money should be in the Income Bucket and the Growth Bucket, as described below.

## The Income Bucket

This bucket will hold all our fixed-income investments, such as a bank CD or highly reliable, investment-grade bonds. We will use these funds as the means of regularly (perhaps every three months) refilling our Cash Bucket.

Fixed-income investments, such as bonds, are a great back-up for our Cash Bucket, because they are essentially IOUs. We are letting others use our money for a fixed period of time, during which they promise to provide us regular interest payments, and then return our principal. Their promise to pay is secured by either their overall financial strength, or by specific assets (like property or buildings). These vehicles provide a much better return than cash, yet may (such as a US treasury bond) have virtually no risk of monetary loss. We do give up some liquidity – the ability to have instant access to all the money. Thus, we might visualize this bucket as one containing both ice cubes and water, with the water representing the periodic (perhaps every three months) cash flow being thrown off by the semi-frozen investment.

This bucket had been highly favored by retirees. This was because CDs and investment-grade bonds had provided a good yield, and bonds even increased in market value as interest rates dropped. (When interest rates drop, older bonds are more valuable than newer bonds because they yield greater income for that type of bond than the newer bonds.)

However, things are different now. Overall CD and bond yields are low and market interest rates are expected to rise. When interest rates rise, the older bonds have less value than the newer bonds. The combination of low yields and rising interest rates can even sometimes result in an overall negative total return for bonds.

To deal with these market conditions, many income investors have converted to shorter length bonds, which are less susceptible to the negative effects of an interest rate rise. They've also converted investment grade bonds to other income producing securities, such as high dividend stocks, or high yield (sometimes called "junk") bonds.

Investors always have the option of holding on to their bonds until maturity, at which time they will receive the principal back. However, in that case, a market rise in interest rates will result in an "opportunity cost" (they could have gotten a higher return with the new interest rate), rather than an actual cash cost.

One other point: rising rates will eventually provide more cash returns in future CD or bond purchases, so eventually any small market or "opportunity" loss will be offset by the increase in yields. For example, if rates go up 2% for a recently-issued 5-year bond, in 5 years the investor will no longer have any market loss on that bond, and will be getting an additional 2% return when she purchases a new bond.

How much of your investing money should be in the Income Bucket? Enough to allow you to periodically refill your Cash Bucket for approximately 10 years. Continuing with the earlier example, let's say you retire with $1.25 million in investment money. If you need to maintain $50,000 in the Cash Bucket, you would conservatively target about $500,000 for your Income Bucket. That said, your target amount for the Income Bucket could be reduced by these factors:

- Your number of years of anticipated retirement. The closer it is to 30 years, the closer you should be to the 10-year allocation. However, if you delay your retirement, and have fewer expected retirement years, you can perhaps have an 8 or 9-year allocation.
- The percentage of your annual spending covered by essentially guaranteed payments such as social security and pensions. The higher this percentage, the smaller the required amount in the Income Bucket.
- The relative market conditions for fixed-income securities compared to equity securities. When the overall expected annual returns for bonds are on the low side, you may want to temporarily reduce the amount in the Income Bucket.
- Your personal comfort in living with a bit of risk. If you are not much of a risk-taker, you may wish to hold to the 10-year allocation. However, if you are willing to trade a bit of controlled risk for higher overall investment returns, you may wish to move some of the targeted money for the Income Bucket into the Growth Bucket, described in the next section.

## The Growth Bucket

Your Growth Bucket will contain equities, such as bank or industrial stocks, that will grow in value and likely provide cash dividends. We will use these funds regularly (perhaps every three months) to refill our Income Bucket, which in turn can be used to refill our Cash Bucket. Dividends are particularly helpful for retirees, who can either use them to purchase new CDs or bonds in the Income Bucket, or who can move them directly to the Cash Bucket.

Unlike bonds, equities provide us no promised regular returns. But over time, they will provide greater returns than bonds or other fixed-income securities. Their value is based on the continuing cash flow from dividends and projected capital gains, both which usually increase over time.

Equities are somewhat "frozen" assets that are not easily liquidated, or as reliably converted into cash. With their potential for high growth comes a potential for possible loss, especially in the short run. This can occur when the company profit comes up short, and the shortfall is projected to extend over a long period. Or the loss can occur from a general market decline.

However, this downside to stocks can be mitigated by using our 3-Bucket investment framework. Since we have approximately 10 years of projected spending covered by our Cash and Income Buckets, we have the time to wait out market declines, and pick a better time to sell individual stocks. While waiting for the stock market to go up, we do benefit from the continuing flow of dividends into the Income Bucket. If you keep this in mind, you should be a lot less worried about the inevitable stock market fluctuations. (For some detailed examples as to how the cash flow actually moves between the buckets, see Part 3.)

How much of our investing money should be in the Growth Bucket? Because it is the bucket with the greatest long-term investment returns, after filling up our Cash and Income Buckets, it should contain all of the rest of our investing money.

You always have the option of cutting back on the recommended amount in the Growth Bucket. However, before you make this reduction, keep in mind the benefits of using the suggested bucket allocation with the recommended strategies discussed in the previous three chapters. Using those strategies:

1) All your basic living expenses will be sufficiently covered by a continuous, guaranteed cash flow;
2) You will have enough cash to cover all your expenses for one full year;
3) Your Income Bucket will give you a cushion of about 10 years during which all your expenses will be covered by a highly reliable cash flow;
4) In a down stock market, you will not be required to sell any stocks for a period of 10 years. (The worst "bear" market declines of 20%+ typically last about 2-3 years);
5) Your Growth Bucket will provide the funding for the "nice to have" things, as well as the basic income that will be needed for an extended retirement period.

## The importance of getting your bucket allocations right

There is no simple formula or "average" that can determine the best asset allocation for every individual. You have to go through the basic analyses that we have done in this and the preceding chapters, adjusting the results for your individual circumstances. But this will be time well spent: The consensus among financial professionals is that your asset allocation is the most important decision that you can make. In other words, your selection of individual securities or funds is secondary to the way you allocate your investment in stocks, bonds, and cash - this allocation will be the principal determinant of your investment results! So it is crucial to put a lot of thought and effort into getting the best allocation possible. The 3-Bucket framework gives you the best approach to accomplish this essential work. The next chapters will help you fine-tune your allocation decisions.

## Chapter summary

This chapter has given you a useful framework through which you can achieve a better view all of your retirement financial assets. The most important feature of this 3-Bucket framework is that fixed-income assets can provide you with a 10-year buffer from having to sell stocks during major market downturns. This approach allows you to enjoy higher returns from stock ownership, while protecting you from their major risks.

The next chapter will spell out the returns we can expect from the bonds and stocks that are within these buckets.

# Chapter 5: How can we calculate future returns from investments?

*In these times, calculating future investment returns is a bit like trying to put a value on your house while the kitchen is on fire.*

In this chapter, I will explain how I arrived at the projected 30-year investment returns, and suggested withdrawal rates, used in this book. We'll look first at my projection of inflation, then look at projected bond and stock returns for the next 30 years.

# Inflation and interest rate predictions

Let's begin by looking at my outlook for a couple of key economic measures.

## Inflation prediction

While it is difficult to accurately predict inflation over a long period, I believe it is reasonable for our planning purposes to use the Federal Reserve target rate of 2% inflation per year. If inflation does rise above 2%, both the fixed-income and equity markets should make offsetting adjustments. Thus, when I describe security returns as "inflation-adjusted", they are adjusted for an average of 2% inflation.

## Interest rate prediction

I believe that the US 10-year treasury bonds will generate a "real", or inflation-adjusted 2% return. While this is higher than the current real rates – due to the extraordinary central bank policies that have created abnormally low rates – it is somewhat lower than the historical real rate (2.4%). So I will be using this 2% expected real treasury rate as a proxy for the general investment-grade bond returns.

## Equity return prediction

After reviewing a recent 60-year period of the S&P 500 returns, and considering the most likely future scenarios, I believe that equities will conservatively yield an inflation-adjusted 6% annual total return. There will, of course, be large variation in these returns over annual and 10-year periods, but over the 30 years, the average return should be at least 6%.

## Combined stock/bond return prediction

Based on the preceding, an investment portfolio of 50% stocks and 50% bonds should be expected to produce an average real return of 4% over the next 30 years; a portfolio of 60% stocks and 40% bonds should yield a real return of 4.4% during that time period. These predictions assume that the investor will not be selling stocks during periods when the market experiences a drop of 20% or more (a "bear" market).

# Calculation of returns in varying economic conditions

Projected interest and stock return rates will vary in different economic conditions, but due to their typical inverse relationship, the combined rate will be fairly consistent. For example, in a recent 12-month period, the interest rate was about the same as the inflation rate, yielding a 0% real return for bonds. In the same period, stocks had a real return of 8%. So for that period the blended 50/50 stock/bond rate was 4%, consistent with my general expectations, in spite of the varying individual components of the combined rate.

# Returns reduced by investment fees and taxes

Increasing numbers of investors use indexed mutual funds or ETFs to invest much of their bond and stock money. If the investor uses these funds, the annual expense associated with their investments can be as low as .10 %, which will have a minor effect on their returns. In contrast, actively managed funds can have expenses in the 1.0% to 1.5% range, which will have a huge negative effect on their returns. In this case, the investor will need to get a substantially higher return (than index fund returns) in order to justify the much higher expenses.

## Taxes also will affect net returns

Depending on the type of financial security and the type of account it is held within, there will be taxes on the returns from your investments. This will, of course, lower your net return – just as income tax and social security taxes have lowered your net income throughout your working career. Subsequent chapters will give suggestions as to how to lower these taxes.

## Sources for the calculations

These rates were synthesized from a number of sources, and included past, present, and anticipated future rates. I reviewed historical rates, weighing the more recent years more heavily; I considered the present rates currently being used by CFP® professionals actively working with clients; and I studied research on future rates as published in the Financial Planning Association Journal.

## These projected return rates are consistent with recent reports that endorse the validity of the 4% withdrawal rate guidelines

It is always a challenge to get projected returns just right, but the methods described above produce a result that is consistent with recent studies and reports (*see* Part 3). As those studies confirm, a 50/50 stock/bond portfolio would support a 4% average withdrawal over a 30-year period. As discussed in the previous chapter, I am advocating that you use a dynamic planning model to make sure you can successfully navigate a period with a below-normal returns. Part of the dynamism comes from the use of fixed-income funds to buffer the portfolio from poor stock returns. The other part of the dynamism comes in making small adjustments to the annual withdrawals, to help compensate for unusual volatility of returns.

## Chapter summary

This chapter explains the reasonable, conservative investment return rates used in this book. They are based on historical rates, current conditions, and a best-estimate of likely future economic conditions.

In order to simplify the understanding of projected returns, I have rounded off the calculated projected return rates used in this chapter. These round numbers should make it easier for the investor to more frequently make the checks and subsequent adjustments necessary for a consistently successful financial plan.

# Chapter 6: Retirement planning applications

*To learn from your mistakes, you must realize that you are making mistakes.*

Let's now apply the techniques covered in the first five chapters to a fairly straightforward situation, using large round numbers to make it easier for you to translate this application to your own situation. Our purpose is to see how the ideas fit together, and to see the potential mistake involved in allocating too little of your portfolio to stocks.

We'll look at twin brothers Bob and Bill. Bob will follow the recommended investment asset allocation of 50-60% stocks; Bill will use an ultra-conservative asset allocation of only 25% stocks. All other facts about their financial situation will be identical, including having no mortgage on their homes.

## Example using a recommended stock allocation

After tallying up all his past and expected expenses, Bob determines that he will need $100,000 per year in retirement. He and his wife will be receiving $45,000 per year in social security, plus a small pension of $5,000, which has an annual inflation adjustment. In addition, he will have total retirement investments of $1,250,000, plus $40,000 in cash. Bob multiplies his investments by 4%, arrives at $50,000, adds in his social security and pension, and determines that his overall expected income comes to $100,000 – a match with his expected expenses. So far, so good!

Next, Bob adds up his basic living expenses, which amount to $60,000. He adds up his guaranteed cash flow, and it comes out to $50,000, or 83% of these expenses. Since at least 75% of his basic expenses are covered, if Bob was willing to accept a bit of risk, he would be okay; however, being somewhat concerned with this issue, he decides he'd like to increase his guaranteed cash flow. He uses $250,000 from his investments to buy an inflation-protected immediate annuity that will cover himself and his wife. The annuity pays $10,000 annually, so now Bob has all his basic living expenses covered by guaranteed cash flows.

Bob has $40,000 of discretionary expenses – covering important activities such as trips to see his grandkids, golfing, gifts to family members, donations to church and charities, new clothes, dinners out, and vacation trips. Bob decides to invest $400,000 in a total bond fund (within his Income Bucket), and $600,000 in a total stock fund (within his Growth Bucket).

Bob will start his retirement with $40,000 in his Cash Bucket, and can be confident that he will receive $60,000 guaranteed cash flow throughout the year. Thus, all of his expenses for next year are covered.

Each quarter, Bob will transfer $10,000 from his Income Bucket to his Cash Bucket. If the Growth Bucket has posted an increase in the quarter, Bob will likewise transfer $10,000 from it to the Income Bucket. If not, Bob will skip making the transfer until there is an increase during a future quarter. At that time, Bob will make the transfer, and restore the Income Bucket to its full $400,000 level.

Once a year, Bob will consider making a few adjustments to this plan. He will compare his budgeted expenses to his actual expenses, and determine if there should be changes to his spending or investment plans. He can also make an inflation adjustment to his withdrawal plans. Finally, he should review the level of the Income Bucket – if there has been no transfer due to a continuing drop in stock prices (perhaps due to a 10% "correction" or a 20% "bear" market), he should set the stock price level at which the quarterly withdrawals should resume (perhaps at the level the correction or bear market was identified).

By making these regular transfers among buckets, Bob will always have his next year's expenses fully covered by cash. He will also maintain an approximate 10-year cushion of bonds to replenish his Cash Bucket. He will still have the majority of his investment money in the higher long-term return Growth Bucket, yet will usually not be required to sell stocks during the inevitable market corrections, and will certainly be able to wait out any bear markets.

## Example using an ultra-conservative stock allocation

Bill will have the same pension and social security income as Bob. He will also have the same retirement money and cash. In order to fully meet his basic living expenses, he decides to buy an immediate annuity. Thus far, his financial plan is exactly the same as his twin brother Bob.

Like his twin, Bill now has $1,000,000 to invest. However, unlike his brother, Bill makes just a 25% stock allocation in his portfolio and then buys bond funds with the balance. The resulting combined return will yield only about 3% per year. So Bill will be able to safely withdraw just $30,000 to cover his $40,000 in discretionary expenses.

So what is Bill to do? As described in Chapter 1, Bill could find a way to increase his income, such as some form of a retirement job. Bill could also reduce his discretionary expenses (fewer rounds of golf, no visit to see grandchildren, no vacations, etc.) Or he could do some combination of income increases and expense reductions.

Or Bill could reconsider his investment allocation – and perhaps follow his twin brother's 60% stock allocation. With that scenario, Bill will not have to worry about a retirement job, nor have to make tough expense decisions (such as fewer rounds of golf versus not seeing grandchildren).

To become more comfortable with his increased equity allocation, Bill also might want to consider the backup options to his investment returns (as we'll discuss in the upcoming chapter on risk management). For example, he could safely convert his home equity into income through a newer form of a reverse mortgage line of credit.

## Chapter summary

This chapter demonstrates how to use the recommended investment allocation strategies in this book. It also shows that you can always take an ultra-conservative approach to financial planning – but then you will probably need to make spending adjustments to compensate for the lower income. Only you can judge the relative value of this trade-off.

The next chapter will describe the specific securities you can use to build your investment portfolio.

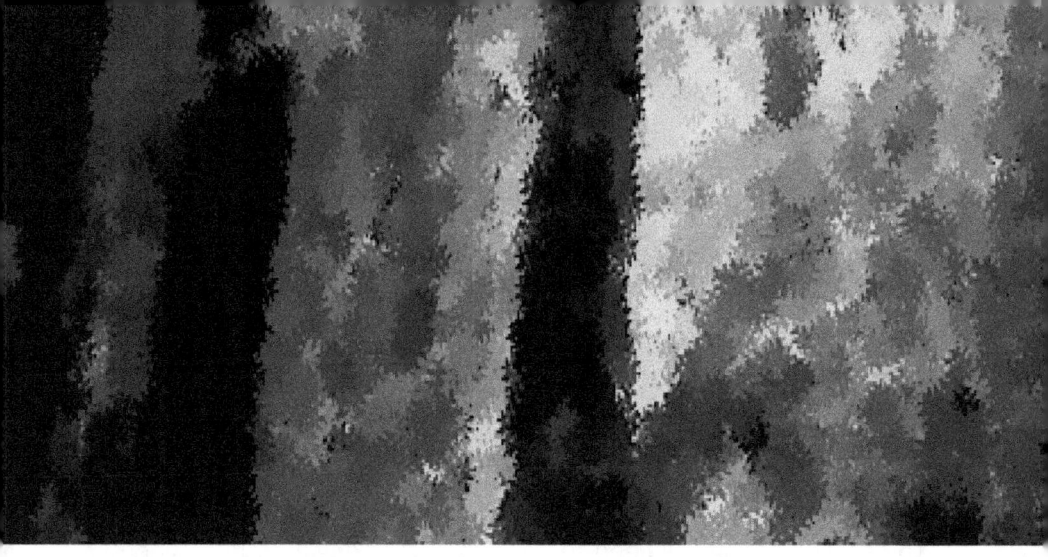

# Chapter 7: Which are the best financial securities for me?

## (Or: How should I fill those buckets?)

> *Investor: Where should I invest my money?*
> *Advisor: Booze. Where else can you get forty percent?*

Let's now look at the best investment vehicles within the buckets explored in previous chapters. We'll look at options for each bucket, and then discuss some options that could help fill more than one bucket.

Please note that this listing will not include every possible option, but it will survey the most important investment vehicles for people beyond 55.

## Cash Bucket

As discussed in the earlier chapters, you will need enough cash such that, when combined with your continuing cash flow, you will be able to cover 12 months of expenses. The question is: Where to park that cash?

To begin with, you will need some form of checking account – whether at a bank, a credit union, or at an investment services company.

Banks are the traditional choice for checking accounts. They generally will have the widest range of account options to choose from. They have had the most experience with online bill paying, and they usually have customer-friendly systems. They also tend to have the most flexible account features, including a variety of ways of transferring cash to other financial institutions (such as cashiers' checks). Their accounts are insured up to $250,000 by FDIC, a US government agency.

Credit unions provide good alternatives to standard bank checking accounts. Because they have lower overhead costs, they can provide checking accounts at a lower cost and with a somewhat higher interest rate. All federally-chartered and most state-chartered credit union accounts are insured up to $250,000 by NCUA, a US government agency.

Brokerages and other investment services companies usually offer checking accounts as well. Besides using their checks, you can often get cash from a debit card at ATMs. A key advantage of this option is to consolidate most or all of your financial transactions with one company (like Merrill Lynch, Morgan Stanley, or Fidelity Investments). The checking account funds may be insured by the FDIC if the money has been deposited in a bank. If the cash is in a money market fund, it is not guaranteed by the government, but is still quite safe. For a more detailed comparison of investment service companies to banks, see Part 3.

Regardless of the checking account you choose, you will want to make sure that you get the best possible interest rate for your money. Ideally, you will have an account, especially at a bank, that will automatically move or "sweep" a high balance into another, higher interest account. If this is not possible, you have a number of other choices to consider. You could put excess cash in a 6-month CD at a bank; or in a money market fund at a credit union; or in a short-term bond fund at a brokerage.

## Fixed-Income Bucket

You will use the regular cash flow from this bucket to refill the Cash Bucket. Let's look at the best sources of this cash flow.

### Total bond funds

One simple vehicle to use for your Income Bucket is a low-expense (as low as .10% yearly at Vanguard and Fidelity) index mutual fund that covers the entire US bond market. Typically, total bond funds are designed to provide broad exposure to US investment grade bonds. They generally invest about 30% in corporate bonds and 70% in US government bonds of all maturities (short, intermediate, and long-term issues). Because the funds invest in all segments and maturities of the fixed-income market, you can use these funds either exclusively to handle the Income Bucket, or can use them as your core income vehicle in a portfolio of bond investments.

 Pluses: You will have a much diversified investment, and thus will be protected from losses arising from specific issues with individual company or sector bonds. The mutual index fund expenses are rock-bottom low; this is an especially important factor in today's low-interest environment. You will usually get a higher return than you would from a similar mutual fund that is actively-managed rather than indexed.

 Minuses: You will be unable to adjust to certain macro-trends in the economy, such as rising interest rates triggered by the Federal Reserve.

## Sector bond funds

You can also purchase mutual funds or ETFs (Exchange Traded Funds) that contain specific sectors or types of securities, such as foreign bonds, government bonds, or utility bonds. (For a discussion of the advantages of ETFs compared to mutual funds, see Part 3.)

Pluses: Each sector fund provides unique advantages. Foreign bonds provide additional diversification beyond that provided by the US total bond funds. US government bonds have the highest possible protection against default. Utility bonds have a higher interest rate than the broad bond market.

Minuses: All of these funds will have a greater annual expense than the total bond fund. Foreign bonds may add an additional risk factor, such as instability of the governments. Having sector funds would reduce the diversification provided by the total bond fund.

## High yield or "junk" bond funds

These funds offer a high interest yield to compensate for their poor risk rating (BB or lower). The companies issuing these bonds may have some trouble paying interest or redeeming the principal.

Pluses: Over time, these bonds generally will provide a greater return than the investment grade (rated higher than BB) bonds. Any individual bond default will be offset by all the other bonds that do not default, especially when the economy is improving.

Minuses: These bonds can be problematic in a deteriorating economy. The bond prices have a volatility similar to stocks, thus the bonds don't have the same diversification effect against stocks as do investment grade bonds (which "zig" when stocks "zag").

## Short-term bond funds
These are bonds that have a short maturity – perhaps 1 or 2 years.

Pluses: You are "locked in" to an interest rate for a short time. This would tend to reduce losses in a rapidly rising interest rate environment. You will get your principal back in a short period of time, minimizing risk of default.

Minuses: The interest rate is relatively low. In a falling interest rate period, money will have to be reinvested in a lower interest rate.

## Long-term bond funds
These are bonds that have a long maturity – perhaps 15, 30, or more years.

Pluses: The interest rate will generally be greater than that of shorter maturity bonds. In a falling interest rate period, you will be able to retain the higher interest rate for a much longer time.

Minuses: These bonds can be risky in a rising interest period, as you are locked into a rate that rapidly is eclipsed by the rates of new issues of a similar-maturity bond. When this happens, investors prefer the new bonds, and the market will "discount" the old bonds by establishing a lower market price. Even if an individual personally holds these bonds until maturity, the person will suffer an "opportunity loss" - meaning that they would have been unable to take advantage of new higher market rates.

## Municipal or tax-free bonds

These are bonds issued by state or local governments that are free of federal income tax.

Pluses: They can be advantageous to the high-marginal income tax payer, resulting in an overall higher after-tax return.

Minuses: Interest rates are lower than similar non-municipal bonds.

## Individual government bonds

These could range from savings bonds to individual 10-year or 30-year treasury securities.

These can also include treasury inflation-protected securities (TIPS). The principal of these bonds is adjusted upward or downward each month with changes in the inflation rate. The periodic interest payment thus effectively increases or decreases with changes in inflation.

Pluses: You can have a high level of confidence that you will get your interest and your principal back. If you hold them to maturity, you will receive all monies promised on the bond. You save annual fund expenses.

Minuses: You will have more processing, paperwork and tax reporting as compared to holding these in a mutual fund.

## Individual corporate bonds

These are bonds issued by an individual company, and can be purchased directly from the company or through a broker.

Pluses: You have more control over the investment, as compared to a deposit in a fund. If you hold the bonds to maturity, you will receive all monies promised on the bond. You save annual fund expenses.

 Minuses: If purchased through a broker, you will pay a fairly substantial commission. You will also have more processing, paperwork, and tax reporting than you would have with a similar fund. You also will have less diversification than a bond fund. If there is a problem with one of the companies, and there is a default, it can have a significant impact on your finances.

## Bond ladder

A bond ladder is a portfolio of bonds with a portion of the portfolio maturing each year (often equal amounts across each annual maturity). A bond ladder can be as short as two years or as long as 30 years or more. For example, you might initially buy maturities of 1, 2, 3, 4, 5, 6, 7, 8, 9, and 10 years, and then as they mature, replace each with a 10-year note.

 Pluses: You minimize risk. Simple bond ladders, particularly maturities of 10 years or less, did not experience annual losses any time over the past century. As the potential for rising rates looms, a simple bond ladder may be one of the best approaches for fixed-income investing.

 Minuses: If purchased through a broker, you will pay a fairly substantial commission for each bond. You will also have more processing, paperwork, and tax reporting than you would have with a similar fund.

## Growth Bucket

You will use the substantial return from this bucket to provide most of the money needed to meet your retirement goals. Let's look at the best sources of this return.

### Total stock funds

One good way to fill the Growth Bucket is to purchase low-expense index mutual funds or ETFs that cover the entire US or world stock markets. These funds attempt to replicate the broad market by holding the stock of every security that trades on a certain exchange, or invests in a certain country or the world as a whole. When buying these funds, you often track a broad index such as the Wilshire 5000, Russell 2000 or MSCI US Broad Market. As an alternative, you can also replicate the entire world market through such funds as the Vanguard Total World fund (VTWSX).

Pluses: You will have a diversified investment, and thus will be protected from losses arising from specific issues with individual or sector stocks. The mutual fund expenses are rock-bottom low (as low as .10% yearly for total US stock funds at Vanguard and Fidelity; Total World is higher, around .30%). You will usually get a higher return than you would from a similar mutual fund that is actively managed rather than indexed.

Minuses: You will have no flexibility to adjust to certain macro trends in the economy, such as the current rising interest expectations, as fueled by planned actions of the Federal Reserve.

## Sector stock funds

You can purchase mutual funds or ETFs that contain foreign stocks, or specific sectors, such as technology, medical industry, or utility stocks.

Pluses: Each sector fund provides unique advantages. Foreign stocks provide additional diversification beyond that provided from the US total stock funds. Certain sectors will do better in a rising economic cycle (e.g., the technology sector), some in a stable economy (e.g., the medical sector) and others in a falling economy (e.g., the utility sector). Some sectors have higher dividend rates (utility sector); others usually have a higher stock price growth.

Minuses: All of these funds will have a greater annual expense than the total stock fund. Foreign stocks may add an additional risk factor, such as instability of the governments. Adding other sector funds would reduce the diversification provided by the total stock fund.

## Individual common stocks

You can use a broker to purchase and sell individual shares of the ownership of a company.

Pluses: You will have the greatest control over your Growth Bucket. You might be able to purchase an individual stock at a bargain price and then sell it when it becomes overpriced. You might choose to hold an individual stock for a long time and effectively avoid taxes on capital gains until it is sold. You will pay no mutual fund expenses.

Minuses: You might have to live with tremendous volatility in the stock price. Individual companies can become bankrupt or go totally out of business, and you can lose the entire value of the stock shares.

## Preferred stock

This is a hybrid security that offers a fixed dividend, and usually has an option to convert it to common stock at some time in the future at a predetermined exchange ratio.

Pluses: You will receive a higher current yield than most stocks. You will also usually be granted an option to convert your preferred stock to common stock, with certain conditions.

Minuses: Unlike with common stocks, you will have no participation in the earnings growth of the company. You will also have less security of income than you would have with bonds.

# Diversification and alternative investments

One of the great advantages of having both stocks and investment-grade bonds is that they tend to move in opposite directions: When one is up, the other is usually down. When economic conditions are improving, stocks usually go up due to increased profits and cash flow; but then bonds will often go down because the rising economy leads to more demand for borrowed money. That causes rates to rise, which in turn causes existing bond prices to drop. The opposite effect happens when the economy is declining: Stocks go down while bonds go up. This offsetting diversification can take a lot of the volatility out of your overall investment returns, which in turn allows you to get a better night's sleep.

Alternative investments can provide additional diversification to further reduce volatility. Here are a few that you may wish to have a minor role in your investment portfolios.

## Real estate

You might consider purchasing investments such as a real estate fund or a REIT (Real Estate Investment Trust), like the Vanguard REIT ETF (VNQ). Often these kinds of investments can be used as an alternative for the

Income Bucket, since most of the dividends come from sources like office rentals. Their cash flow will have a somewhat different pattern than that of a typical bond fund. These investments can also go up with inflation, thus they can provide a hedge to help minimize the effect of inflation on your portfolio.

## Gold

If you are concerned about rising inflation, you might consider putting a small percentage of your investments in gold. You could, for example, invest in SPDR Gold Shares (GLD). Like real estate investments, gold investments are based on a physical substance that will go up with inflation. However, unlike with real estate, gold does not have any intrinsic wealth-producing characteristics (e.g., nobody pays you rent for holding gold). Gold investments, as with other precious metal investments, can often have volatile prices. Therefore, you would want to be cautious about making any substantial investment in this area.

## Options

When you own an individual stock, you can use options to provide additional income or to act as a hedge against a large drop in stock value. When you create a call option, you receive a premium, which is useful in situations where you believe that the stock will not rise much in value. When you purchase a put option, you can protect a stock position against a major loss in value. The put option pays off when the stock price drops to a specified level. This is obviously useful when you are concerned about volatility in the stock market, yet do not want to sell a specific security at the current time. While they can be very useful, options used incorrectly (especially so-called "naked options", which you can create without owning shares) can be extremely risky. You should have a financial advisor help you with an options investment.

# Investments for both the Income and Growth Buckets

You can use certain investments to at least partially fill both the Income and Growth Buckets. Let's look at several of these.

## Balanced funds

A balanced mutual fund is one that contains both stocks and bonds. Three good examples of a balanced fund are the American Funds "Income Fund of America" (IFA); Vanguard's "Wellington Fund"; and Vanguard's "Wellesley Fund". Each has a different percentage of bonds: IFA – 25%; Wellington – 35%; and Wellesley – 63%. Each of these is considered to be a very good core holding for investors of any age, but particularly for those of retirement age. Over the last 10 years, these funds have averaged an inflation adjusted 5-6% return per year, and their annual dividend payments to investors have averaged about 3%.

A retiree could conceivably fund all of her Income and Growth Buckets with one of these balanced mutual funds. However, a better approach for most people would be to use these funds to form a core of both buckets, and then use other securities to fund the balance of the buckets.

Pluses: In general, the fund expenses are low. Fund managers are able to select stocks and bonds most suitable for providing consistent income with some growth in share values. The managers can vary their allocations to take best advantage of varying market conditions. They can also emphasize sectors that will have the best likely returns.

Each fund will have its own particular advantages. For example, IFA will usually provide a higher dividend yield because it has a higher portion of stocks and high yield bonds. The Vanguard funds have lower fund expenses and no purchase "load" (or commission).

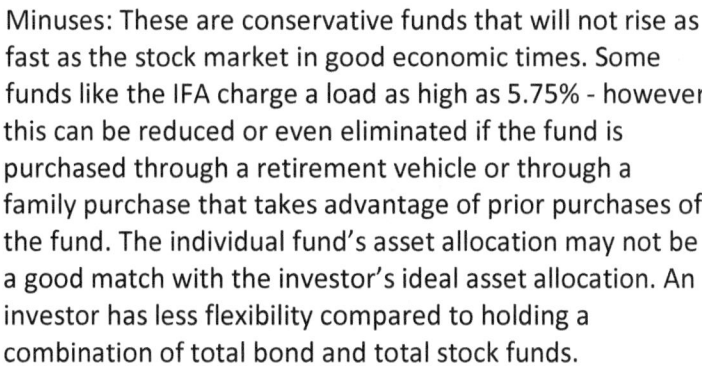

Minuses: These are conservative funds that will not rise as fast as the stock market in good economic times. Some funds like the IFA charge a load as high as 5.75% - however this can be reduced or even eliminated if the fund is purchased through a retirement vehicle or through a family purchase that takes advantage of prior purchases of the fund. The individual fund's asset allocation may not be a good match with the investor's ideal asset allocation. An investor has less flexibility compared to holding a combination of total bond and total stock funds.

### Life-cycle funds

Life-cycle or target-date funds contain stocks and bonds that vary in proportion to an investor's age. Typically, as the investor ages, the stock portion goes down and the bond portion goes up. This continues until the investor reaches age 65.

Pluses: This can be viewed as a "set it and forget it" decision for a younger investor that does not want to spend any time analyzing his or her own particular financial circumstances. The fund helps you avoid gross mistakes like having all bonds at age 30 or all stocks at age 60.

Minuses: This standardized method for allocating portfolio assets may be fine for many investors, but may be a poor match with your own situation. Also, the allocations do not shift past age 65 – thus providing little value for those who are already past that age.

## Buying income and growth securities

Some of the options, such as the Fidelity and Vanguard funds, can be purchased directly from the respective companies. Other options, such as those from the American Funds, must be purchased through a broker. You have the following strategies to consider using, depending on which options you are interested in, how comfortable you are with these options, and how much you want to get involved in researching other choices.

### Do it yourself
If you decide to go with the simplest option, total bond and total stock index funds, one account with either Fidelity or Vanguard would do the trick. You won't need professional help. However, if you decide to pursue other options, such as owning individual stocks or bonds, you will likely need to open additional accounts, and you will need more assistance.

### Get a little help
If you wish to go with a combination of options, and are not fully comfortable with doing this on your own, you may wish to open an account with a full service brokerage firm such as Fidelity, Morgan Stanley, or Merrill Lynch. While naturally partial towards company offerings, their sales representatives and advisors can provide some helpful assistance. You might also consider seeking out a local bank that offers these services.

### Get lots of help
If you wish to get some investing assistance within the context of a complete financial plan, you can hire an independent financial advisor who can help you select the right securities, and have the investments fit within the context of an overall financial plan. Beyond investment management, this plan would include such important considerations as taxes, insurance, and estate planning.

## How safe is my money?
This is the Bernie Madoff question: What's the chance of someone stealing my money? In order to answer this question, let's look at two areas: the mutual funds themselves and the brokerage houses.

## Mutual funds

By law, mutual funds are kept in a trust fund within a bank, separate from the management unit of the mutual fund. The mutual fund itself is required to have several independent directors on its board. It is also required to send audited annual reports to the Securities and Exchange Commission (SEC), and all reports are available to investors.

## Brokerage accounts

These funds are insured up to $500,000 by SIPC, a brokerage insurance company established by the industry. SIPC covers the possibility that a brokerage firm may become insolvent, or the possibility of account theft or unauthorized trading. Large financial intuitions such as Merrill Lynch, Morgan Stanley, and Fidelity have "excess SIPC" coverage from an insurance company that can cover amounts up to one billion dollars. This coverage applies to their custodial function with all accounts at their firm. Brokers must send audited annual reports to the SEC.

## The answer to the "safety" question

If you have your investments in large, established mutual funds, and housed in custodial accounts at large financial service companies, your money is protected against fraud. Of course, all monies in non-guaranteed accounts are subject to a potential wide variation in value due to issues within individual companies and due to general fluctuations in the market.

If you are working with small, newly-established mutual funds or brokers, you may not have all the same assurances described above. You will need to do more due diligence to ensure the safety of your money. That typically involves doing some additional research into the fund and its operations, and asking your sales representative or broker specific questions about their firm.

## Should I have more or fewer accounts?

In general, simplicity beats complexity. All other things being equal, it would be a good idea to consolidate your accounts and financial institutions wherever possible. For married couples, joint accounts often make more sense than individual accounts. 401(k) accounts from past employers can be consolidated into one IRA. Mutual funds can be transferred from one large financial institution (like Morgan Stanley) to another one (like Fidelity). In fact, for some it may make sense to have all financial accounts, even checking, housed at one institution.

However, you also might find that it is not possible or even advisable to consolidate all accounts, or to transfer everything from one financial institution to another. For example, IRAs for two people cannot be combined, nor can you have a joint-account IRA. You might have an account in TIIA-CREF that has no precise equivalent in Fidelity. You might be able to transfer a Vanguard account to Fidelity, but would have to pay transaction fees that would not occur if you left the account at Vanguard. You might find that retaining an account might provide you with research privileges that would be lost if it were transferred to another institution. For estate planning purposes, some remarried people with children from a previous marriage might be better off with individual rather than joint accounts.

So the bottom line is: Deciding on the right number of accounts and financial services firms will depend on many factors, which you should be ready to consider and discuss with an independent financial advisor.

## Chapter summary

This chapter gave a detailed look at the financial securities you can consider as you fill each of your 3 buckets. It also provided the potential advantages and drawbacks of several different kinds of investments that might be used in more than one of the buckets.

The next chapter will consider some optional ways to fill the Income Bucket in the current economic environment.

# Chapter 8: Possible modifications to your Income Bucket

*What did the big bucket say to the little bucket?*
*You look a little pail!*

Some investors might like the basic 3-Bucket approach, yet wonder if a modification or two in the Income Bucket makes sense for them. This chapter will take a look at several common substitutions that you might consider, namely:

- High dividend stocks
- High yield ("junk") bonds
- A balanced fund

## Can I replace bonds with high dividend stocks?

Bonds recently have had such a low annual return that many investors are looking for alternatives. One common alternative considered is a high-paying dividend stock. Investors see that a total bond fund pays a 2% dividend, but AT&T common stock pays a dividend of 4-5%. Why not sell bonds in the Income Bucket and replace them with high-dividend stocks? The short answer: It can be risky to make such a swap. To see why, and to make your own informed decision on this issue, consider the differences in cash flow associated with this possible exchange.

Dividend cash flow is really a hybrid of "reliable" and "variable" cash flows. Individual stock dividends can be reduced or even suspended in bad economic times. Thus, for a group of diversified dividends, we can normally count on 75% of the flow to be reliable, but the other 25% should be viewed as variable. As a result, in order to have the same reliable cash flow as the bonds, we need to replace the bond income with least 25% more income from dividend stocks.

If you make such an exchange, you should follow these guidelines in order to reduce the risk to an acceptable level:

1) **Do not swap out all of your bonds.** You should keep at least 50% of your Income Bucket comprised of investment grade bonds – because these will retain a high level of income reliability and will also retain a minimum level of diversification for the portfolio as a whole. Remember, under the 3-Bucket system, we may sell more of our bonds in times of a general stock decline. If we overly-replace our bonds with high dividend stocks, junk bonds or a balanced fund, we may not have the bonds to "protect" us from having to sell our stocks in a bad market.

2) **Watch out for very high dividend yields.** Dividend percentage yields are based on the market value of the stock, and if the stock is in financial trouble, the market price drops, and the calculated percentage yield will (usually temporarily) go up. In this situation, a dividend cut (or worse) is often on the horizon for that stock.

3) **Use a highly diversified selection of dividend-paying stocks.** This will substantially reduce the impact of company-specific or industry-specific non-payment of the dividend.
4) **Be patient with a temporary drop in overall dividends.** The S&P 500, a highly diversified group of stocks, had its worst dividend income drop since 1960 between 2008 and 2009, when it experienced a 20% drop. Three years later, however, the dividends had fully recovered, and the drop had been erased.
5) **Balance added dividends against added risk.** Because of the potential risks, you should consider only <u>75%</u> of your total diversified stock dividends to be as safe as the interest from investment-grade bonds.

Following these guidelines, an investor who has a 50/50 bond/stock portfolio, and who is willing to take on a bit more risk, could convert her portfolio to one comprised of 35% bonds/20% high dividend stocks/45% total market stocks. The high dividend stocks should be diversified; should have good financial metrics (such as a good trend in earnings and cash flow); and should include a number of the "dividend aristocrat" companies (those with a long record of maintaining and increasing dividend payouts). You also might want to consider a fund that specializes in high dividend stocks.

## Can I replace my investment grade bonds with high yield bonds?

High-yield, or so-called "junk" bonds, are those issued by less creditworthy companies. In order for these bonds to be attractive to investors, they must have a much greater interest rate than the bonds issued by a financially strong company. In the current period of ultra-low interest rates, some investors wonder if they should replace their investment-grade bonds, issued by financially strong companies, with the high yield bonds from less financially stable companies.

There is an obvious risk to making this change – especially if you purchase individual bonds. If the company, or the general economy, experiences hard times, some of these junk bonds will default. That means that they will eventually not pay some or all of their obligations. This risk can be mitigated by buying these bonds in a fund, rather than through individual purchases. However, some default risk will remain, with the possible result that the overall bond yield and fund price could go down substantially.

The less obvious risk is that junk bond prices tend to move more like stock prices than bond prices. Thus, as discussed above with dividends, the substitution of junk bonds for investment bonds will lower the diversification in your portfolio, and you will be less able to compensate for stock market drops.

On the positive side, the junk bonds will have a higher long-term return than investment-grade bonds. If you and your portfolio can handle the additional risk, it could be worthwhile to substitute up to 10% of your investment-grade bonds with junk bonds. This swap would be especially worth considering if there is an unusually large disparity between the yields.

## Can I replace my bonds with a balanced fund?

Balanced funds seek to provide the investor with a reasonably steady "fund dividend." These dividends are mainly provided from the fund's bond and stock dividend income.

Many retired people like these funds because of their regular payout. With their diversified, conservative holdings, these funds are able to provide a consistent, and sometimes increasing, source of income for retired investors. While the balanced fund dividend is somewhat less reliable than that of investment grade bonds, it will be more reliable than income from stock dividends.

So should you replace your bonds with a balanced fund? There is a problem, as discussed earlier with the other two bond substitutes: Even though a balanced fund is a diversified security, you will lose some overall diversification in your portfolio. You will be substituting a combination of stocks and bonds to replace your bonds, thus lowering both your bond percentage and your ability to adjust to a poor stock market period.

However, a balanced fund can have a legitimate place in your total portfolio. Here's how to think about it: The balanced fund has its own, self-contained, 3-Bucket system. Unfortunately, the breakdown of the fund's buckets will probably not exactly meet your best allocation of asset classes. However, if you really like the balanced fund idea, you can put up to half of your investment money into a balanced fund, and then invest the rest in a combination of stocks and bonds that eventually results in your best investment allocation. This would require a bit of work: You would have to calculate the percentage of bonds in the balanced fund, and then make sure that you have the right amount of other bonds to arrive at the proper percentage for your overall portfolio.

## Chapter summary

Bonds and treasuries do much more than simply provide income. They provide an important diversification to other asset classes – like stocks – so that our total portfolio has much less volatility. That, in turn, encourages all of us to stick with our investment plan in stressful times.

Because of the current economic times with such low interest rates, many income-oriented mutual funds have cut back on their investment-grade bonds and increased their dividend-paying stocks and their junk bonds. An individual investor who is considering mimicking this strategy must be fully aware of the risks involved in such a shift, and should take the steps suggested in this chapter to mitigate these risks.

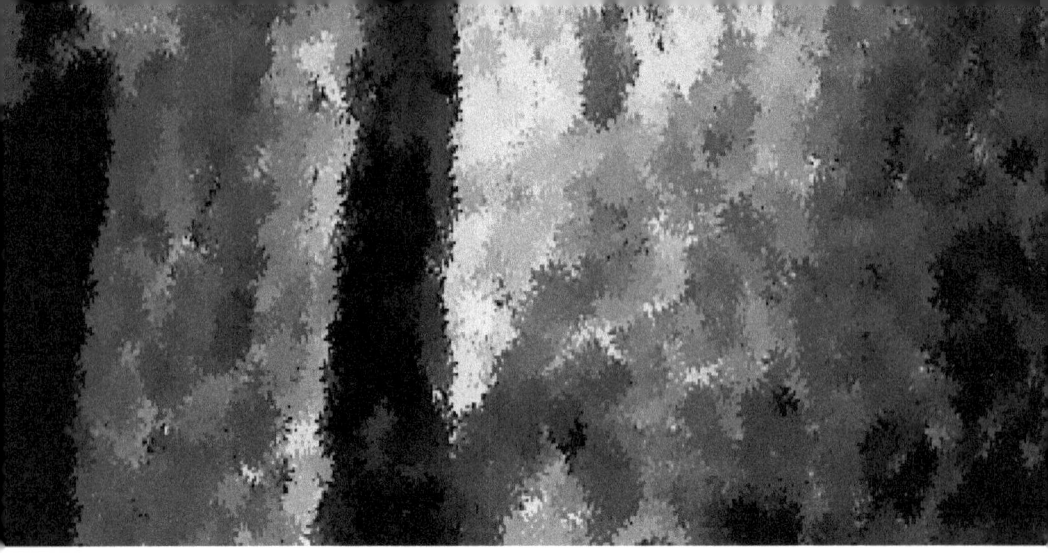

# Chapter 9: Tax-advantaged individual pension accounts

*A fine is a tax for doing wrong. A tax is a fine for doing well.*

## What are individual pension accounts?

The US income tax code often severely punishes us for trying to use regular bank or investment accounts as a means of saving money for retirement.

Consider someone in the 25% tax bracket. Each paycheck dollar, after deducting $0.25 in taxes, will net only $0.75 to invest. The interest on this $0.75 investment is then taxed at 25%, resulting in only $0.56 – little more than half of the paycheck dollar! - available to do the actual work of generating retirement earnings.

In contrast, money in a pension account compounds income tax-free until needed in retirement. And then it is taxed at the marginal income rate, perhaps as low as 15%. So for each dollar of earnings put into the plan, we might have $0.85, instead of $0.56, actually generating earnings. What a difference!

While fewer of us now enjoy the benefits of a traditional pension plan, virtually all of can participate in the alternative individual pension plans such as 401(k), IRA and Roth accounts.

## Types of pension accounts

### Defined contribution plans

You participate in these pension plans at your place of employment. They may be labeled a 401(k) or a 403(b) plan, so called by where they are authorized in the tax code. They are referred to as "defined contribution" plans, characterized by a defined contribution of employer funds to an employee account, one that is managed by the employee. The employee also can make a contribution to the account, money that will not be subject to income tax until it is withdrawn (after age 55 or age 59 1/2) in retirement. These plans differ from a traditional pension plan, where an employer manages the pension money, and then gives you a "defined payment" when you retire.

Let's trace through the benefits of these defined contribution accounts.

To simplify things, I like to think of each of these accounts as comprised of two sub-accounts:

✓ **Your sub-account**, one that will accumulate earnings free of all US income tax – let's call it the "**TF**" (tax free) account; and the

✓ **Government sub-account,** one that will also accumulate earnings, but is deferred and owed to the government – let's call it the "**GOV**" account.

As an example, let's assume you will be in the 25% tax bracket both when you put in and withdraw your money. And let's further assume that you put $133 of your salary into a 401(k) account. The $133 is considered tax-deferred income, because payment of the income tax due on it is deferred until the money is taken out of the account.

So you start with $100 in the your TF sub-account and $33 in the GOV sub-account. If you get a 10% investment return, your TF grows to $110; and the GOV account grows to $36.30.

In comparison, let's say you did <u>not</u> put the original $133 into the 401(k), you just paid $33 in income tax, and then invested the $100 in a regular account and received the same 10% return. You will still get a $10 return, but you will pay a 25% tax, and thus end up with a net income return of $7.50. Compared to putting the money into the 401(k) TF account, your effective return drops from 10% to 7.50%, or a 25% reduction.

This example demonstrates the value of just one year of TF money. Each year you will receive compounding, tax-free returns. When you do finally withdraw money from the 401(k), you simply pay the income taxes by sending in the money from the GOV account – the one that you have been holding technically in your name, but that has always in effect belonged to the government.

Please note that the example assumes you will have the same tax rate when you make and withdraw plan contributions. If your tax rate drops in retirement, you will be sending in less money from the GOV account; if your tax rate goes up, you will need to send in more.

When you leave your employer, you generally can keep these accounts with your employer (without being able to make additional contributions), or you can roll them over tax-free to an IRA. This option gives you more control over the account, and may offer more investment choices.

*Traditional IRAs*

Traditional individual retirement accounts (IRAs) are plans similar to 401(k)s, but are set up and controlled by individuals rather than companies. IRAs can be established with a bank, brokerage firm, or mutual fund company. In the most common "deductible" version, your contributions are deducted from your income, and put into an account that effectively has the same two sub-accounts as a 401(k): the TF account and the GOV account.

IRA withdrawals prior to age 59 ½ are always subject to a 10% IRS early withdrawal penalty. With the 401(k), if you leave your company after attaining age 55, you will be able to make certain withdrawals penalty-free.

In the "non-deductible" IRA version, your contributions are taxed at the time they are made, but then accumulate tax-free, and are withdrawn tax-free. The non-deductible IRA would be especially useful if you have a low marginal tax rate at the time of your contributions to the plan.

*Roth IRAs*

Roth IRAs are individual accounts in which you pay income tax on contributions, but then receive both tax-free growth and tax-free withdrawals. In this sense, they are similar to a non-deductible IRA. Roths are, however, much more flexible than standard 401(k)s or traditional IRAs, especially as to when you can (or must) withdraw money without penalty. With the other individual accounts, you must begin to make minimum required distributions (MRDs) when you turn 70 ½. With the Roths, there are no MRDs. Roths are also better for estate planning, as they can provide beneficiaries tax-free income for a longer time. For these reasons, Roths are usually the last-tapped source of money for retirees.

Because most people highly value the up-front tax reduction, they will generally have most of their tax-sheltered account money in traditional IRAs. However, Roth IRAs can be especially useful if you already have maxed out on your traditional IRA contributions, anticipate a higher marginal tax rate in retirement, or wish to gain the flexibility discussed in the preceding paragraph. Chapter 11 will review some of the finer points in creating an optimal blend of traditional and Roth IRA accounts. The balance of this chapter will focus on the best use of the more common traditional IRAs.

## How can I best use traditional IRA accounts to lower my taxes?

It can be a challenge to determine the best way to lower your taxes with these individual accounts. Let's say that you want to allocate your investments between a regular brokerage account and a traditional individual retirement account. Here are a few of the issues and conflicting considerations:

Issue: Should you put interest-bearing securities into your IRA? Considerations:

- Interest payments will have the highest <u>percentage</u> of taxes minimized by the account; but
- Interest payments are at historically low levels, so the interest <u>amount protected</u> might be small.

Issue: Should you put stocks in your IRA? Considerations:

- Stocks will usually have a much higher total return than interest payments, so the <u>amount protected</u> might be large, however,
- Depending on your marginal income rate, stocks usually have a lower-than-interest <u>percentage</u> (0%, 15%, or 20%) that is taxable.

So let's say you have four types of securities: utility stocks, small company growth stocks, a total bond fund, and high-yield bonds. Which should be put into an IRA?

Most people should:

- Put the high-yield bonds in the IRA, but put the high-dividend utility stocks outside of the IRA.
- Put the high-growth small company stocks in the IRA, but put the low-interest total bond fund outside the IRA.

As these questions and answers suggest, if you really want to get the best returns with your IRA, you will need to do a detailed analysis of the effective tax rate for each of your securities, and then choose the scenario that gives you the best after-tax return.

Your situation actually becomes simpler when you start to withdraw funds in retirement. You must have the flexibility to be able to withdraw varying amounts of stock and fixed-income funds, such that you do not get stuck withdrawing from a fund that has had a major drop in value. This becomes especially critical when you begin to take MRDs at age 70½. Thus, the best way to use the IRAs at that point is to have them mirror your overall asset allocation. So if your overall allocation is 60/40, Stocks/Bonds, your IRAs should also have the same 60/40 allocation.

## What should I <u>not</u> put in my IRA?

You should not consider putting anything from the Cash Bucket into an IRA. The withdrawals from a traditional IRA would generate unneeded taxes and paperwork. You would also save little, if anything, and would waste the IRA space that could be used for long-term investments.

Tax-free municipal bonds should absolutely not be put in any tax deferred accounts like a traditional IRA. All income distributed from a traditional IRA is taxable, even if it is tax-exempt when earned. Therefore, you would up be paying income tax on a bond that is "tax-free," and has a lower interest rate than a similar taxable bond.

Annuities issued by insurance companies should not be put into an IRA. Because an annuity already provides a tax deferral for income earned, using the annuity in an IRA is duplicating the deferral aspect. In other words, you would be putting a deferred product inside a deferred account. And since there are added administrative expenses connected with the annuity, you are reducing your investment growth, as compared to simply holding investments similar to those that underlie the annuity in your IRA.

## Chapter summary

This chapter discusses the best ways to take full advantage of your tax-deferred accounts. As suggested in the chapter, these decisions can be fairly complex. To make the best decision, you will probably need to do a substantial analysis of your investments, either by yourself, or with the aid of a CFP® professional.

The next chapter will discuss recommended investment portfolios.

# Chapter 10: Recommended investment portfolios

*Money talks. Trouble is, mine only knows one word - goodbye.*

As described in Chapter 4, you will be using the money from your Growth Bucket to refill your Income Bucket, which in turn will be used to fill up your Cash Bucket. In Chapter 7, we focused on the investment securities that tend to do the best job for you within each bucket. In this chapter, we will take a more comprehensive view, and consider the *combination* of specific securities that would best work with all three buckets.

There are many potential combinations to use, and your best combination will be dependent on your goals, your risk tolerance, and your cash flow needs. This chapter will discuss the best portfolios for the majority of those beyond 55.

We'll begin with the three key criteria that should be used in evaluating investment portfolios. We'll then use these criteria to evaluate a number of potential portfolios. The three criteria are:

## Growth in net value

In order to cover your expenses now and in the future, you will need a good net return from your investments. This net return is comprised of the gains from payments of interest and dividends, plus the increases in market value; and the reductions from commissions, fund expenses, and the like. You'd like to maximize the gains, consistent with your goals, while minimizing the expenses.

## Consistency in cash flow

Since you will be using your investments to replace at least some of your previous job-related income, you will need a consistent cash flow from the portfolio.

## Minimization of risks

You will want to avoid a couple of risks. First, you would certainly prefer not have any total financial losses, as in bankruptcies and bond defaults. Second, you would like to minimize both individual security and fund price volatility. These risks are especially concerning in the years immediately leading up to, and following, an individual's retirement.

Here are my recommended portfolios for you to consider, listed in order of their simplicity to set up and manage:

## Portfolio 1: Total bond and total stock funds

How to do it: Based upon your analysis from Chapter One, put all Income Bucket funds in a total bond fund, and put all Growth Bucket funds in a total stock fund. You should pick from the broadest index funds – those that cover the most individual securities – and have a low annual expense ratio (.05 - .10%).

Advantages: Over the long run, this portfolio will produce a higher net value than one composed of actively-managed funds that have higher expenses. It will also produce a relatively-steady cash flow from interest and dividend payments. Because there is little buying and selling within the funds, they are tax-efficient. The funds are highly diversified, thus eliminating individual security and sector-specific risks. The combination of stocks and bonds further increases diversification and lowers overall expected price volatility for the portfolio. You can easily adjust the percentage of stocks and bonds to deal with changing personal or market circumstances.

Disadvantages:  You will be unable to fine-tune your investments to include specific individual securities or sectors.  You will not get the highest possible net value, the maximum possible annual cash flow, or the lowest possible volatility within each of the buckets. (You will, however, usually get a better combined result on these criteria than most other portfolios.)

## Portfolio 2: Add a balanced fund

How to do it: Put half into a balanced fund (such as Wellington, Wellesley, Income Fund of America, or Capital Income Builder). Put enough of the rest into total bond and total stock funds such that you achieve your desired split between the Income and Growth Buckets.

Advantages: This portfolio will produce a higher cash flow from interest and dividend payments than the previous portfolio. Because there is limited buying and selling within the overall portfolio, it is relatively tax-efficient. The portfolio is fairly diversified, with some concentration in the more cash-producing securities. You can consider using the higher cash flow from fund dividends to help refill the Cash Bucket. This is particularly helpful when bond yields are low. The professional fund managers will assume the task of security selection and allocation into asset categories within the balanced fund.

Disadvantages: If you use the added dividends to replace the cash coming from the Income Bucket, you will be assuming additional risk. There will be more annual fund expenses. You may be charged an up-front "load", or purchase commission, by some of the balanced funds. The process of changing your percentages of stocks and bonds is more complex than with Portfolio 1.

## Portfolio 3: Add bond and stock sector funds

How to do it: Use Portfolio 2, but replace some of the index funds with sector funds.

Advantages: This portfolio will tilt your investment results in the direction of the sector funds you purchase. For example, if you add a utility ETF, you will increase your cash flow, but you will lower your expected net growth. And if you add a high-yield bond fund, you will increase your cash flow, but also increase your volatility (and therefore your risk). If you add international stocks or bonds to US index funds, you will increase diversification, and you may lower your volatility.

Disadvantages: There will be more fund annual expenses. You will find changing the percentages of stocks and bonds to be more complex than with Portfolio 2.

## Portfolio 4: Add alternative investments

How to do it: Use Portfolio 3, but replace some of the index funds with tangible investments such as real estate investment trusts (REITs), gold funds, or commodity options.

Advantages: This portfolio will be more diversified, which should lower the overall price volatility of your portfolio.

Disadvantages: You will likely lower your long-run net value growth. For example, REITs can be a good alternative cash flow, but they do not have the same tax advantages as dividends. Gold can be a great hedge against inflation, but it has no inherent mechanism to increase wealth, like stocks do. You will also find it challenging to keep the bucket amounts in optimal balance.

## Portfolio 5: Add individual stocks and bonds

How to do it: Use Portfolio 4, but replace some of the funds with individual stocks or bonds.

Advantages: Individual securities will have no annual expenses, like funds do. You will have more control over the makeup of your portfolio. You can take advantage of any unique information you have learned or developed about a specific security, which may help you increase the net growth of the portfolio.

Disadvantages: This will lower the diversification in your portfolio, and will thus likely increase volatility and risk. You will also risk the complete failure of the individual security.

## Chapter summary

Creating your ideal portfolio combination can be a complex process, one that needs to consider the general goals for any portfolio, as well as your own personal goals. This chapter began with a good, simple "set it and forget it" portfolio, and then proceeded to cover other, more complex options that might be more appropriate for your individual goals.

After selecting an ideal portfolio, you will need to convert your existing portfolio to your new one. The next chapter will give you several ways to accomplish this conversion.

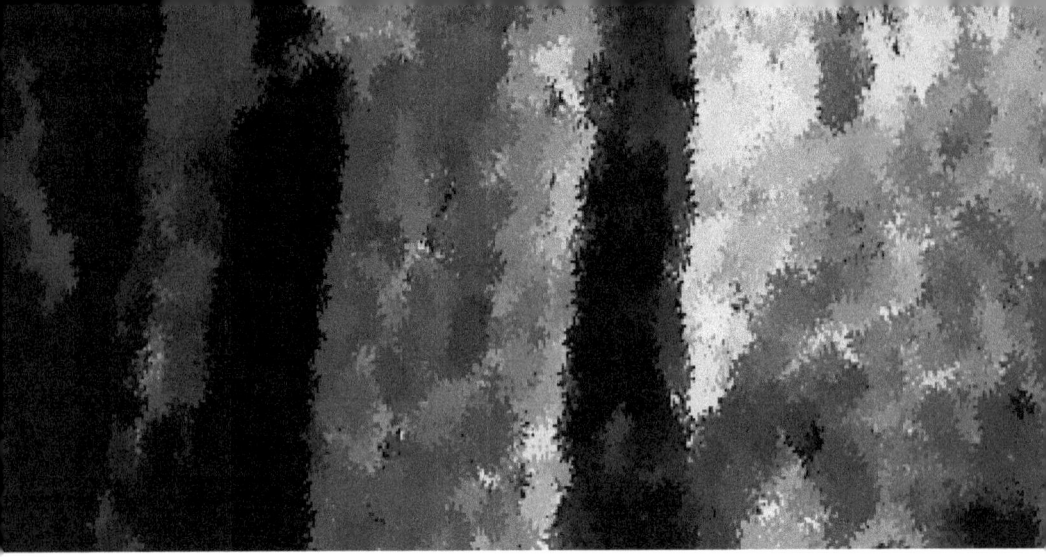

# Chapter 11: Making your portfolio more effective and tax-efficient

*"I've got all the money I'll ever need, if I die by four o'clock." – Henny Youngman*

## Implementing a more effective portfolio

After considering the previous chapter, let's say you wish to make a change to your investment portfolio. For example, you now wish to have 60% in a total stock fund, and 40% in a total bond fund. How should you go about making this change?

We'll look at several broad options to accomplish this conversion to a more effective portfolio.

## Sell everything, then buy the new funds.

This is the simplest way to get to your target portfolio. You can sell portions of your holdings over a period of time (e.g., 25% per quarter), and then buy the new funds. In this manner, you will minimize the risk of selling in an overall poor market. With some individual investments, such as specific bonds in a temporary low-interest period, you might want to accelerate the selling schedule; with other investments, such as stocks that have been depressed because of sector-specific economic conditions, you might want to extend your selling timeframe.

You also need to be aware of the expense and tax consequences of this approach, and then find ways to mitigate any negative consequences. For example, some mutual funds and variable annuities have selling fees, especially if the security has not been held for at least a minimum period of time. So you should seek to hold these for a period long enough to avoid these fees. If selling generates short term capital gains, you could avoid the tax by waiting to sell the security until the timing creates a more-favorable long term gain. And if the capital gains are substantial, you may wish to spread the selling over a 2 or 3-year period to avoid pushing into a higher marginal income tax bracket.

## Analyze your existing portfolio; keep some, sell some.

You will first compute a ratio of how much of your current investments are stocks and how much are bonds (or fixed-income). To do this, break down each investment into one of these categories, add up each category, and divide by your total investment to get the percentage of each asset class. Most financial service companies have calculators that can assist you with this analysis.

Based on these numbers, you will know how much to be shifted from one category to the other. For example, if you have too many stocks, you can sell off the excess, and then buy a total bond fund. You would then have a portfolio that is pretty similar to your target, with a minimum of work.

An advantage of this conversion method is that it involves less selling than the previous method, so it will have fewer expense and tax consequences. The drawback is that your resulting total portfolio will probably be less diversified than if it were all total bonds and total stocks.

## Do a complete analysis, see how it matches your spending, then make changes.

The previous two methods might be called the "quick and dirty" ways to make the conversion. The third method will take more time, but will usually be more effective and efficient than the other methods. It will allow you to retain securities that may actually enhance your targeted portfolio.

The first step will be to do an overall stock/bond ratio analysis, as described in the previous method.

The second step is to do an investment cash flow analysis for the next 10 years. As you may recall, the cash from our fixed-income bucket creates the "buffer" that protects us from having to sell our stocks at an inopportune time. So if we have $400,000 in our target portfolio for that buffer, we would want to see how our current, reliable cash flow compares to that target.

The third step is to determine the diversification of your current holdings. For example, as compared to your target portfolio, are you overly-concentrated in one industry? Do you have too many large stocks, or too many growth stocks? Many financial service companies have analytical tools that can be of considerable help. However, you will likely need to do much of this work yourself.

The fourth step is to examine each individual security in light of the analyses in the previous three steps. You will also will want to compare the returns and annual expenses of the security to the returns and annual expenses of your target portfolio securities.

The fifth step is to sell off the securities that make your portfolio less diversified, have more expenses, or have a poorer expected return than your target portfolio securities. You then use this money to purchase the replacement securities or funds that are consistent with your optimal portfolio.

As you may realize, there is a substantial knowledge base and a considerable research effort involved in this method. If this process is of interest to you, and you have the time to work though the analysis, you can likely do this on your own. As an alternative, you may wish to hire a CFP® professional to do some or all of this work for you. If this interests you, see Chapter 14 for information as to how to connect with a financial planner.

## Creating a more tax-efficient portfolio

As we have discussed in this chapter, tax considerations do play an important role in our investment decisions. This section will extend that discussion to the best use of tax-sheltered individual pension accounts and other strategies to reduce taxes.

### Tax-sheltered and tax-free accounts

As discussed in Chapter 9, the greatest advantage of 401(k)s, traditional IRAs, and Roth IRA accounts is that they allow us to accumulate and compound our money income-tax free until needed in retirement. When we are near or in the early part of our retirement, we have several decisions to make concerning these accounts:

- Should we add to these accounts?

  This is an option if either you or your spouse continues to work – even in a part-time job. But if you do add to the accounts, will you then have to take money for living expenses from another tax-sheltered account? If so, there would be little value in adding to a tax-sheltered account. On the other hand, if you have most of your investments in fully taxable accounts, it would make sense to add money to your tax-sheltered accounts, and take living expenses from the taxable account.

- Should we convert our 401(k)s to IRAs?

When you leave your employer, you generally have the option to keep your 401(k), or roll it over tax-free to an IRA. If you are at least 55 when you leave your employer, you might choose to not roll it over, and begin penalty-free distributions from that 401(k). On the other hand, if you do convert it to an IRA, you must wait until 59 ½ to begin penalty-free distributions. However, IRAs give you much more account control, and more investment options, than 401(k)s. Plus you no longer have to be concerned about your former company's administrative procedures or choice of pension trustee. So, on balance, most people find it is a good idea to convert to the IRA.

- Should we convert our traditional IRAs to Roth IRAs?

Roths have some advantages over traditional IRAs. Roth plans are much more flexible, especially as to when you can (or must) withdraw money without penalty. With the other individual tax-advantaged accounts, you must begin to make minimum required distributions (MRDs) beginning when you turn 70 ½. With the Roths, there are no MRDs. Roths are also better for estate planning, as they can provide beneficiaries tax-free income for a long time.

When you convert to a Roth, you must pay income taxes on the deferred income within the IRA; however, if you can use money from a regular investment account to pay the taxes, you substantially increase the amount that is now tax-free. An example may clarify these points:

*Example*
You have $20,000 in a regular investment account, and you are paying 25% tax on all its income. You also have $40,000 in a traditional IRA. (Thus, you likely have only $30,000 of tax-free money; the rest will eventually be paid as income tax when withdrawn). You decide to convert the IRA to a Roth account, and use $10,000 from the regular investment account to pay the income tax due. Your entire $40,000 from the traditional IRA, now in a Roth account, becomes tax-free! On the other hand, if you had chosen instead to use $10,000 from the IRA

to pay the income taxes involved in the conversion, you would only have merely transferred the $30,000 of tax-free money from the traditional IRA to the Roth.

So far, the conversion of $40,000 to a Roth IRA looks good if you are able to use regular investment money to pay the income tax. However, it might be a bad idea if some or all of these items apply:

- You have to pay capital gains taxes when you sell your securities;
- Your capital gains tax will be lower in a future year because your other income will drop;
- You have to pay additional income taxes because the conversion puts you into a higher marginal tax rate; or
- There will be a drop in your future overall income tax rates.

In other words, you will need to carefully examine your current and future marginal income tax rates. If your top income tax rate will likely drop in the future, you may not want to make this conversion; on the other hand, if your marginal tax rate will likely rise, it would be better to "lock in" the current lower rate by making the conversion to the Roth account.

For more details on these conversions, see Part 3.

## Using tax-advantaged securities outside of IRAs

When considering these traditional IRA and Roth decisions, remember that some securities in regular investment accounts are also tax-advantaged, including:

- Municipal bonds, which are typically free of federal income tax (although their interest rate is typically below the general bond market rate);
- Dividends, which can have a federal income tax rate of 15% or even 0%
- Growth stocks that are held for a long time, for which the capital gains tax (currently 20% or less) is assessed only when

the stocks are actually sold. In this circumstance, the increase in the stock value can be sheltered for a long time. In fact, if the stock is transferred through an inheritance, the tax basis price is "stepped-up" to the value at the time of the inheritance, thus eliminating any capital gains tax for the beneficiary.

## Chapter summary

This chapter has given you optional ways to make your portfolio more effective and tax efficient, especially within the recommended portfolios discussed in the previous chapter.

At some point you will be withdrawing funds from your portfolio. The next chapter discusses the most efficient way to go about that process.

# Chapter 12: In which order should I tap my retirement funds?

*I'm spending a year dead for tax reasons. – Douglas Adams*

This chapter will discuss the order in which to withdraw funds when in retirement. These will be the funds you will use to replenish your Cash and Income Buckets. In general, the best order is the following:

1. Interest and dividends from securities that are in regular investment accounts;
2. Fixed-income securities (like bonds) that are in regular investment accounts;

3.  Stocks that are in regular investment accounts;
4.  Securities that are in tax-sheltered accounts, such as traditional IRAs; and
5.  Securities that are in tax-free accounts, such as Roth IRAs.

This order may need to be modified to better suit your particular situation. This modification would be based on several factors, as listed below.

## Income and Growth Buckets factor

As part of the 3-Bucket strategy, you will be withdrawing money from your Income Bucket (usually bond) securities every quarter. Then, if there have been positive stock returns, you will be replenishing your Income Bucket from the Growth Bucket. In this situation, as a practical matter, you will be making both a fixed-income (bond) and a growth (stock) withdrawal.

On the other hand, if stocks have had a large negative return, your withdrawal will be totally from fixed-income securities. This will continue until stock returns become positive, and the bucket allocations are rebalanced.

## Minimum required distribution (MRD) factor

Upon turning 70 ½, you will need to make an IRS-mandated MRD from your IRA/401(k) accounts. The MRD percentage withdrawal is based on your age; at 70, it is approximately 3.5%. So as a practical matter, after 70 ½, you would begin your withdrawal strategy with your MRD, then follow the other guidelines for withdrawals.

You should be aware that the government exacts a heavy penalty if you don't make this MRD – currently, there is a 50% excise tax on unpaid MRDs. Additionally, while you can lump all of your IRA accounts together, and take one MRD on the combined balance, you will need to take a separate MRD from each 401(k) account. For more details on the best ways to handle MRDs, see Part 3.

## Income tax bracket factor

When you have a variety of retirement accounts (such as regular investment accounts, traditional IRAs, and Roth IRAs), you may be able to time your withdrawals to pay substantially less income tax. For example, let's assume you are near retirement. You expect to be in the 25% tax bracket in retirement, and yet you make little job income over this calendar year, so you are currently in the 15% bracket. In this case, you may want to withdraw extra money from your traditional IRA in order to take advantage of your temporary lower marginal tax rate. In other words, if you can get away with paying a 15% tax rate on an IRA withdrawal this year, why pay a 25% rate next year?

Here is another example that shows how to take advantage of varying marginal tax rates:

Let's assume that the Browns – a married, retired couple – have their assets in a variety of different retirement accounts, and they plan to withdraw $70,000 from the retirement accounts to cover their income needs for this year. Should the Browns make their withdrawals from the traditional IRA or the Roth IRA account? If they blindly follow the order of withdrawal suggested at the beginning of this chapter, they would take all of the money from the traditional IRA. However, a smarter withdrawal might come from a combination of the two accounts.

Let's assume they limit their traditional IRA withdrawal to $53,900, and their net taxable income increases to $75,300—the top of the 15% bracket for 2016. They then withdraw the remaining $16,100 from their Roth account.

This saves the Browns $4,025 in taxes this year, compared with just withdrawing everything they'll need from the traditional IRA. This savings is $1,610 greater than if they used the Roth in a year in which their marginal income tax bracket was 15%. The same tax saving tactic could be accomplished with other tax-free income sources, such as a regular savings account. Alternatively, if they had cash-value life insurance, they might have been able to use a policy loan instead of a withdrawal from a Roth IRA. Regardless of which tax-free source used, this tactic also preserves their ability to withdraw the traditional IRA money in a future year when their tax bracket may be lower.

A final point on income taxes: Make sure you take into consideration your state's tax laws. Some states have income tax on all income; others, like Illinois, offer favorable tax treatment for certain sources of retirement income, such as 401(k) plans and pensions; and, finally, several states (like Florida) have no state income tax at all.

For more details on managing withdrawal taxes, see Part 3.

### A tool to manage these factors: creating a 10 to 20-year cash flow timeline

As discussed in earlier chapters, in order to make sure that you have the proper withdrawals from your retirement portfolio, you should create a cash flow diagram that might cover 10 to 20 years. This chart could be reviewed and adjusted on an annual basis to make sure your plans remain on track.

This cash flow chart can also be used to work through the factors discussed in this chapter to determine the most tax-efficient way to make your investment withdrawals over an extended number of years.

## Chapter summary

This chapter has given you guidance as to the best order in which to withdraw funds from your retirement monies. Rather than always going with the same order of withdrawals, you should give proper consideration to both the 3-Bucket framework and your marginal tax rates, so that you make the smartest withdrawals.

The next chapter will give you ways to protect your portfolio so that you will be able to withdraw sufficient funds throughout your retirement.

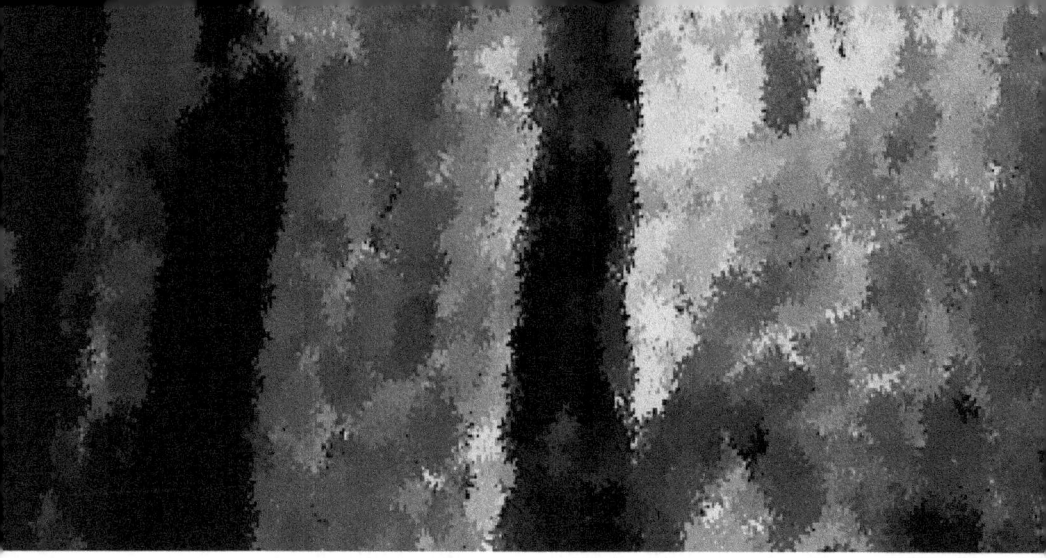

# Chapter 13: Risk management – your plan B options

*An investor to his advisor:*
*Is all my money really gone?*
*Advisor:*
*No, of course not. It's just with somebody else!*

Most likely, you engage in a high-risk activity every day, one that kills over 30,000 Americans each year. And that activity is...driving a car. So why do you do it? Because of the tremendous benefits of driving: the freedom to go where you like, when you like, and get there pretty quickly. Or perhaps you drive because you simply have no other realistic choice.

Because most of us recognize the risk involved in driving, we take a variety of actions (like regular car maintenance and defensive driving) to reduce the chances of being involved in an accident, and we put in place backup plans (such as insurance, and alternative transportation) to minimize the damage if we do have a car wreck.

In many ways, managing retirement funds is similar to driving a car. We use certain risky securities, such as stocks, because of the benefits they give to us. But at the same time, we want to reduce the chances of having a serious problem. And if that problem does occur, we want to have a way to minimize or even eliminate its effect.

My former boss once parked his brand-new Lexus at Chicago's O'Hare airport. When he pulled into a parking area that recently had a number of thefts, I asked: "Bob, aren't you worried about parking in this area?" His simple response: "No...that's why I have insurance." In this chapter, we will discuss investment insurance that can give you that same level of confidence, as well as other "Plan B" options.

Earlier chapters discussed a variety of financial risks that create unwanted volatility in our returns. They included risks related to:

- Type of financial security (e.g., a start-up company stock);
- Company-specific risks (e.g., a poor acquisition decision by the company);
- Sector-specific risks (e.g., the dot-com bust);
- Market shifts (e.g., small market capitalization stocks doing poorly); or
- Economic risks (e.g., an ebb tide in the general financial world that lowers all boats).

However, these earlier chapters also discussed ways you can help prevent or minimize each of these financial risks. They include:

- Having diversified types of securities (e.g., holding both stocks and bonds);
- Having diversification within each type of security (i.e., different stock and bond sectors);

- Having a system that avoids selling stocks at the wrong time (i.e., 3-Bucket approach); and
- Doing an annual review of your overall program results, as well as a check on investment components (e.g., individual stocks and sector funds).

This chapter will focus on your potential back-up plans if a huge unexpected expense comes up, such as a long nursing home stay. It will also discuss ways to cope with extraordinarily negative financial markets.

## How to pay for three years at a nursing home

Many nursing homes cost at least $250 per day, so a three-year stay could cost $250,000 or more. (Medicare does not pay for long-term nursing care; Medicaid will pay, but only for those with investments below approximately $125,000). So, how can we cope with this financial risk?

- A traditional way is to have long term care insurance (LTC). The typical policy will cover 3 years, at a maximum of $150 per day. So having such a policy would cover $165,000 of the $250,000, making this stay much more financially manageable. The big problem with LTC is the premium cost: approximately $3,000 per year for policies beginning at age 65. Individuals with less than $500,000 in investments usually cannot afford the premiums. Individuals with more than $1,500,000 are usually better off to self-insure. Those in between $500,000 and $1,500,000 certainly should take a serious look at the LTC option.
- A second option to cover this unexpected cost is to have a 60% equity portion in your investments, rather than a 50% portion. For someone with $1,000,000, this would represent approximately $150,000 extra over a period of 30 years. This money could be put in an emergency fund to be used as needed for nursing home costs.

- A third option is to purchase longevity insurance. A 65-year old can pay $50,000 for a deferred fixed income annuity and then at 85 receive $40,000 each year for the balance of his life. Over a 30-year retirement planning period, this extra money could cover the cost of a long nursing home stay.
- A fourth option is to consider the FHA's Home Equity Conversion Mortgage (HECM) program. This is a newer form of a reverse mortgage loan, which allows seniors to liquidate their home equity, as needed, without selling their home. The loan is not payable until the owners leave their house or pass away. While reverse mortgage loans have historically been cumbersome and expensive, the HECM program is much more effective, especially with its new "Saver" option. This feature allows seniors to tap home equity in a more affordable way, and still get access to at least 50% of the home value. For example, if you are 72 with a $500,000 house, you can get a HECM reverse loan credit line of $277,000, pay the loan costs of $4,000, and have a net of $273,000 available to cover nursing home or other expenses.

## How to pay for other unexpected but essential expenses

It is impossible to anticipate each and every expense that might come up in retirement. Perhaps you will live an extraordinarily long life. Or perhaps you will incur major legal expenses that are not covered by your insurance plans. What back-up options might you have for these situations?

1. As discussed above, you might consider longevity insurance, especially if a long life runs in your family. As also discussed above, you also should seriously look at the HECM program as a means of withdrawing equity from your primary residence.
2. You also might consider selling nonessential assets, like a vacation home, or perhaps a second or third car. Some of these assets become less useful to us as we get older, so parting with them at that point may be much easier than it would be now.

You might even be able to sell some other assets through consignment shops or through eBay.

3.  Another option, as always, is to eliminate or lower discretionary expenses. As time goes by, we may find that some of the activities associated with these expenses become less important to us. Even if this is not the case, we may simply need to reprioritize our goals to account for this change in our financial condition, while making sure that we can continue with those activities that are the most important to us.

## How to offset extremely poor financial market conditions

The investment and withdrawal plans described in this book (including periodic reviews and adjustments to the plans) should be able to handle almost all market conditions. But what if the worst possible market conditions cause you to miss your expected returns?

> ➤ If you are concerned about this possibility, and yet have a family history of long life, you might seriously consider longevity insurance. Another effective form of longevity insurance is to wait until you are 70 to begin drawing social security.

> ➤ In some circumstances, you can buy another form of insurance called a "protective put" option. This is a financial instrument that allows you to sell a stock if it falls below a previously agreed upon price. This might be used if you have a large holding that would incur substantial capital gains if sold in fear of a large drop in value.

> ➤ If you plan to live in your current house for the rest of your life, the HECM program discussed earlier would be a good option to consider. While many of us might be reluctant to have a reverse mortgage be a part of our basic retirement funding plan, this option could provide security and comfort in extraordinary situations.

## Other ways to help cope with financial adversity

There are several other perspectives – some drawn from personal experience – that can help us cope with financial adversity:

- I consider that only 90% of my total investment portfolio valuation is really mine; the rest is in play with the markets. That way, a drop or market pullback of perhaps 5%, or even 10%, does not concern me. It seems to me to be just normal variation in the market, likely to be reversed fairly soon.
- A drop in the S&P 500 of 20% (at which time the market has a "bear" status) translates to an actual drop in my portfolio of 10%, because of the diversification of my investments. Getting into a bear market is just something that occasionally happens, and it has always been followed by a market recovery.
- A substantial drop in the market may prompt certain investments to go "on sale," which may be a great time to buy them (remember, the one great investment rule is:  Buy low, sell high).
- If an individual stock drops 10% below the overall market, I might consider selling it if something fundamental has changed. An example of this occurred with a small company called Landauer, which had made some poor acquisitions. I was able to cut my losses short by selling the stock. Sometimes this type of selling can get you an income tax break if you have a capital loss.
- Finally, and perhaps most importantly, in trying situations I have consulted with others that are knowledgeable about the market and about my investment goals. No matter how much you think you know about the markets, in tough times it is great to be reassured that you are on the right track. Advisors with a CFP® mark can provide you with appropriate reassurance, as well as help you with related income tax, insurance and estate planning issues.

## Chapter summary

This chapter took a holistic view of ways to manage the risk involved in investments and in our overall financial plan. We first reviewed the ways to minimize the risk within a portfolio, such as taking full advantage of various means of diversification.

We then focused on what to do if, in spite of our best efforts and plans, we run into a problem. A number of suggestions were given, ones that you should carefully review in more detail before implementing. One of the suggestions was to consult with a trusted advisor, such as one with a CFP® mark. The next chapter will go into more detail about how to best work with such a person.

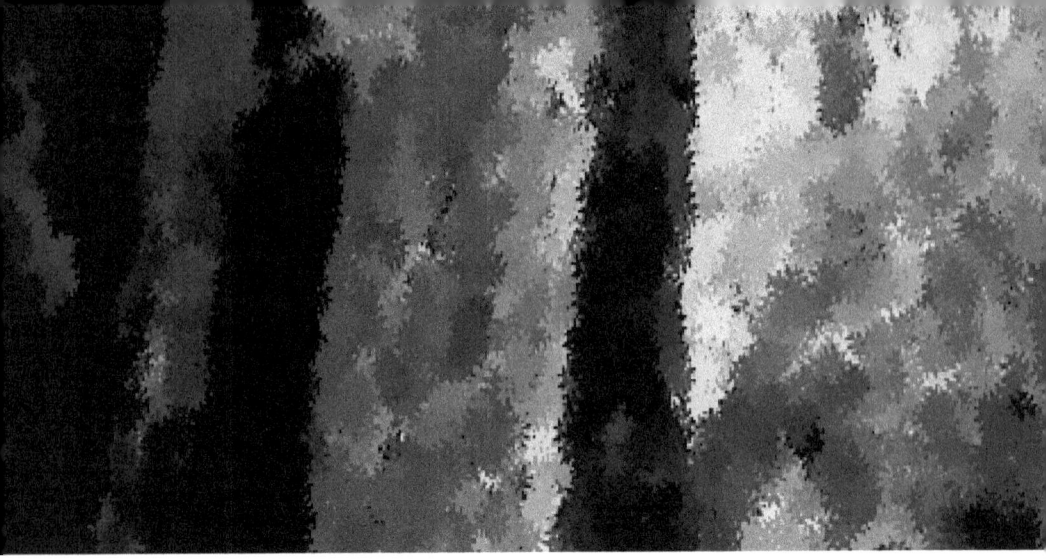

# Chapter 14: Working with financial planners

*FINANCIAL PLANNER - A guy who actually remembers his wallet when he runs to the 7-Eleven for soda pop and cigarettes.*

As suggested in the Introduction to this book, the average investor might be getting only 50% of the available return from his or her portfolio. Thus, if you have a $500,000 portfolio, you could easily be losing out on as much as $10,000 per year!

By following the suggestions in this book, you should be able to substantially improve your investment results. However, if you have some pressing financial questions, would like professional help in creating your financial plan, have a complex financial situation, or would like to make sure that your financial plans fully align, you should seriously consider using a CERTIFIED FINANCIAL PLANNER ™, one that holds the CFP® mark. This chapter will discuss the broad options you have in working with a CFP® professional, how the process works, and how to find a financial planner that best meets your needs.

# Dealing with immediate concerns and planning for your future

As very often occurs, you may first engage a financial planner to help take care of an immediate, pressing concern. If that experience is helpful, you may then use the planner to help develop a more extensive plan that will cover all the key concerns involved in assuring a successful financial future.

## Working with a CFP® professional on your immediate financial concerns

After reading this book, and working through your own initial financial analysis, you may want to have a CFP® professional review your ideas and offer suggestions as to ways to improve that analysis. You also may have questions as to ways to apply the techniques in this book, or perhaps have financial issues that need some quick resolution. Examples of these immediate concerns might be:

- When should I begin receiving social security retirement benefits?
- Should I purchase a particular annuity?
- Should I convert my regular IRA to a Roth IRA?
- How should I best withdraw the required minimum distributions from my IRA?

A good way to resolve these short-term issues is to engage a financial planner on an hourly and project consulting basis. The Garrett Planning Network (GPN) provides an excellent search tool to help you find planners in your area that are willing to work on a limited basis to help you resolve these immediate concerns. See Part 4 for details on to best use the GPN to find your planner.

## Working with a CFP® professional to help achieve your future goals

A common way to work with a CFP® professional is to have him or her create financial plans that will provide you with the guidance needed to help achieve your future goals. To help you create your <u>core financial plan</u>, a CFP® professional will:

1. Identify your goals, the current resources you have to achieve those goals, and the current financial likelihood of achieving those goals;
2. Analyze your investments, then help you realign your investments to better match your goals;
3. Analyze your retirement accounts, integrate these accounts into your investment plans, and make recommendations to help ensure that you will have the cash flow necessary for a comfortable retirement;
4. Review the effect of taxes on various financial alternatives, helping you to select the most tax-efficient plan;
5. Evaluate the most serious risks to your financial plan, then provide alternatives for minimizing the likelihood and potential impact of these risks; and
6. Meet with you on at least an annual basis to review progress or make modifications to your financial plan.

Beyond the core plan, you may require one or more <u>specialized financial plans</u> to deal with concerns like in-depth insurance, tax, or estate planning issues. These plans may involve the special expertise of an insurance agent, a CPA (Certified Public Accountant), or an estate attorney.

## Two planning approaches: flexible and fixed

There are two approaches planners may use to create your financial plan. Depending on your circumstances, you may have a choice as to which approach will be used.

**Flexible** approach

> Here the planner will complete a <u>core financial plan</u> that includes each of the six steps as outlined above. The client remains in control of the process by authorizing the work to be done in a step-by-step process. In a similar fashion, the client will separately authorize any required <u>specialized financial plans.</u> Fees are determined by the actual work done by the planner, not by the size of the investment portfolio.

> Because of the flexibility inherent in this process, virtually everyone is eligible to participate in this approach. As discussed earlier, GPN is an excellent source for planners using this process.

**Fixed** approach

> Here the planner will contract with you to complete a comprehensive plan that includes all of the core and many of the specialized areas. This method may be cost-effective for those with larger sized, more complex financial assets that require frequent monitoring and the potential involvement of a team of specialized professionals. Planners are paid through annual fees, most often determined by the value of client investments.

> If you have investible assets over a million dollars, you generally will have the option to use this approach. The cost of this approach can be fairly substantial (such as an annual fee of 0.5% to 1% of investments), but contracting for a comprehensive plan may be more efficient for some than using the step-by-step, flexible approach.

## How to find a CFP® professional

So you've decided to look for a CFP® professional. Where do you find one?

- Get recommendations from people you trust: family, friends, and colleagues.
- Go to the web sites of the Certified Financial Planner Board of Standards and the Financial Planning Association, which will have a list of qualified CFP® professionals in your area.
- Search the Garrett Planning Network (GPN) for local CFP® professionals. As noted, GPN is an especially good source for planners that follow the flexible approach (discussed above) in developing financial plans.

Part 4 provides details on how to make these on-line searches.

## Should you consider using a financial planner that does not have a CFP® credential?

All financial planners are not created equal. Anybody can say that he or she is a financial planner or financial advisor. But to be certified by the **Certified Financial Planner Board of Standards** -- an organization committed to ensuring that financial planners have their clients' best fiduciary interests in mind -- CFP® professionals have to meet educational requirements and pass a nationwide test. The grueling test (10 hours, spread out over two days) covers retirement planning, investments, insurance and taxation among other topics. CFP® professionals also have to pass an ethical review by the Board of Standards, have a minimum level of client experience, and meet continuing education requirements. The certification must be renewed every two years in order for the individual to call himself a CERTIFIED FINANCIAL PLANNER™ or to use the CFP® mark.

Those legally in the financial planning business are also registered by either the Securities and Exchange Commission (SEC) or by an equivalent state agency.

In contrast, non-CFP® financial advisors have not met all of these requirements. They may be well-qualified to handle certain parts of the financial planning process (like a CPA handling tax issues) but they would not have the comprehensive background of a CFP® professional.

## Why be especially concerned with a financial advisor's compensation?

You should carefully examine the advisor's method of compensation, especially if it is commission-based. The fees of commission-based agents and brokers are tied to specific products and transactions. This compensation model can lead an advisor to overlook what clients specifically need. They may earn commissions on their own products of .55% to 1.25% of their sales, and little if any compensation on competing products. As a result, commission-based advisors often face potential conflicts of interest. For example, mutual funds might be the best investment for you, but your agent-advisor may suggest variable annuities -- because this insurance product will pay her a larger commission.

It is certainly possible to find a good commission-based financial planner, but you will need to perform much more "due diligence" (below) than you would with working with a fee-based advisor, especially one that is a CFP® professional.

## Doing your due diligence in selecting a financial planner

When you have a short list of potential planners, you should first gather information from their web sites, and then have a follow-up meeting with them.

Here are the areas to investigate:

- What are their qualifications? Almost anyone can call himself a "financial advisor". Make sure the person is really qualified to help with your finances. Check for degrees, certifications, and active memberships in professional organizations.

- Do they provide their advice using a *fiduciary standard* (requiring that they act in the <u>best</u> interests of the client, as must be done by a CFP® professional) or a *suitability standard* (requiring only that they provide <u>acceptable</u> choices for the client)?

- What has their experience been? Find out who they've worked with, and what types of planning they've done.

- What is their approach to planning? Everyone approaches finances differently. Find out what kind of planning work this planner most enjoys. If you're looking for advice on a specific problem or financial area, you shouldn't work with a planner who will only develop fixed, comprehensive plans.

- What services do they offer? Finding out what services a planner provides is critical. If you want a planner who can sell you insurance, mutual funds or other financial products, make sure your candidate is registered or licensed to provide those services. As mentioned earlier, a planner, or his firm, must be registered by the SEC or the state in order to give investment advice. Make sure your planner can work in the financial areas that are most important to you. Also, find out who, exactly, will be providing these services. You might be working with other people in the planner's office, too. Make sure you know about all of their backgrounds.

- How will they be paid? As discussed earlier, make absolutely sure you know how your planner will be paid. Does the planner work on a fee-only or a commission-only basis? Is there some other payment arrangement? Remember, some planners have business relationships that could create conflicts of interest. Make sure such relationships are disclosed upfront. If you're paying on a project basis, find out how much you can expect to be charged. Until he or she examines your finances, a planner may not be able to say how much you'll be charged. However, you should be able to get an estimate before any work begins.

- Look into the candidates' records. If the planner does not have the CFP® designation, check with the professional organizations they belong to, and possibly state or federal agencies, for any ethical or legal violations. Once everything is squared away, ask the planner you've chosen to put everything you've discussed into a written agreement that you can keep.

## Chapter summary

This chapter discussed the two major options you may have in establishing a relationship with a planner; an overview of the planning process that a CFP® professional will follow; the advantages of using a planner that has CFP® certification; and the "due diligence" steps you should take, especially when working with a planner who does not have the CFP® certification.

# PART 2

## The Complete Financial Planning Process: Developing and Reviewing Your Plan

Chapters 1-14 addressed the most common and immediate financial question of those beyond age 55: Am I currently on the right track? We reviewed some quick checks to help identify possible problems with your financial plan, then examined some immediate solutions to take care of the issues. I placed these chapters first, because I felt many people in this age group already had some form of a financial plan, and thus would initially be looking for a quick check up on that plan.

But some have never developed a complete financial plan, one that begins with establishing your own value-based goals, and ends with ways to monitor and revise the plan. Others may feel that the plan they have is not comprehensive enough, and perhaps the issues we examined in Chapters 1-14 highlighted some weaknesses in their plan. The next section will help people develop a comprehensive plan, and assist them with a periodic review of their total financial situation. We will use techniques and tools drawn from those I taught to my MBA students as methods for financial and strategic business planning. The more we treat our financial planning in a business-like manner, the less likely we will be influenced by the negative emotions of fear and greed, and the better our results will be. Further, if we are going to take this business-like approach, why not use the most applicable techniques from a graduate school of business?

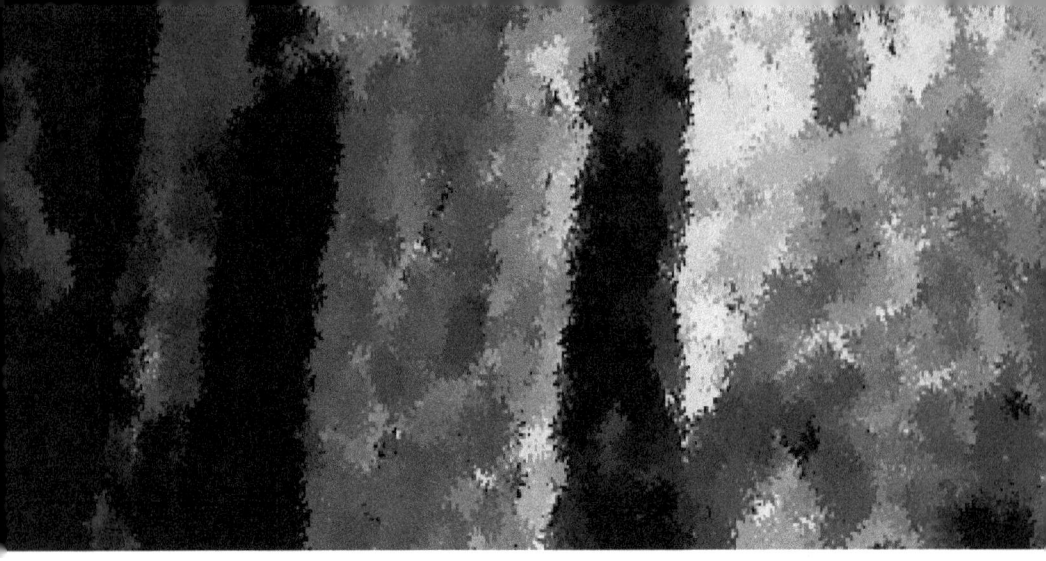

# Chapter 15: Developing and reviewing your plan

*An FBI agent was interviewing a bank teller after the bank had been robbed 3 times by the same bandit. "Did you learn anything from this experience?" asked the agent.*

*"Yes," replied the teller. "He was better dressed each time."*

This chapter will take you through the complete development of a personal financial plan. To make the process as objective and professional as possible, you are going to figuratively leave your home or place of business and be set up in a small office at a nearby strip mall. You are now in charge of a new business called "My Financial Plan"!

Since this is a new business, you will start all the planning from scratch. You will use the following 10 steps to complete your plan.

## Step 1: Create a mission statement

What we are about to do in the first two steps can be exciting – literally helping you create your own future! We'll begin with clarifying what this business is all about by creating a mission statement. Then we will imagine your most desirable future, and put this down in writing as a vision statement.

An example of a good **mission** statement for the business would be:

> *The mission of My Financial Plan is to create an effective financial plan for my retirement that will provide the resources to meet all of my needs, and will provide the financial support to help me achieve all my most important goals.*

## Step 2: Create your vision statement

You should now visualize yourself at least 10 years in the future, with all your needs met and your reasonable wants and expectations fulfilled. After doing this kind of daydreaming, you should create a vision statement for your business.

A good **vision** statement should articulate your wants and needs:

> *As I look ahead over the next 10 to 25 years, I see myself financially secure, checking investment balances no more frequently than once a week, leading a comfortable life, in good health, and engaging in many enjoyable pursuits.*

Feel free to add detail and make as many changes to this statement as you would like – after all, it is your business!

## Step 3: Identify values

The next step is to outline the values that will guide this business. "Values" in this context refers to those things that are most important to you, financially and otherwise. This too can be an exciting activity, because retirement gives us the opportunity to pursue important areas that we simply have not had the time to pursue during our working careers.

Some of these values can be inferred from our vision statement. One value might be the degree to which we seek financial security. Some of us may have a strong desire to never run low on money; others of us may be less concerned about that. In a similar way, some may wish to leave a substantial inheritance to the family; others may not have such wishes. Other examples of values you might have are:

- Participating in extensive vacations
- Spending time in a warm-weather winter home
- Maintaining physical fitness
- Strengthening relationships with family members
- Being significantly involved in grandchildren's lives
- Developing new hobbies or activities
- Participating in charitable activities

After listing these values, you may wish to review your vision statement in order to make sure that the values you have identified can be accommodated by the existing vision. You don't have to explicitly mention all of your values in the vision statement – in fact, it is better if the statement is more concise than verbose. However, you should make sure that the vision statement is consistent with all your most important values.

## Step 4: Use values to create goals

The next step is to use your values to create specific, measurable goals for your business. Goal-setting is one of the most powerful ways for us to influence our behaviors, and to make sure that we achieve and maintain our most important values. Some of our values may require maintenance goals to make sure that we continue to maintain the value; other values may require goals to better specify which growth targets we would like to achieve. Here are a few possible goals derived from our previously listed values:

- I will see each immediate family member no fewer than four times per year.
- I will make sure that all my basic living expenses are covered by a guaranteed cash flow.
- I will maintain a 10% reserve fund as a back up to handle any unexpected expenses.
- By the end of next year, I will have reduced all of my blood chemistry numbers to the normal range.
- Starting next year, I will spend at least 6 weeks, between January and March, in southern Florida.

Goals give us a concrete target to aim for as we seek to achieve our vision and values. Furthermore, the measurement component within the goals will provide us with a means of determining our progress and assessing the extent to which we are on track towards achieving our vision. Therefore, goals help us to become self-motivating in achieving the things that matter the most to us.

Aside from being specific and measurable, goals also need to be realistic. That is, we must feel that with effort it is reasonable for us to achieve them. Unrealistic goals will not be effective in motivating us to achieve them – we may feel that the proverbial hill is too steep to climb, and we may not try very hard to make it to the top.

## Step 5: Compare preliminary goals to current measures

The next step is to determine exactly where the business now stands relative to our goals. For example, related to the value and goal dealing with financial security, you will determine:

- present and future expenses
- the amount of guaranteed cash flow you can expect
- the total amount of investment funds you have
- the breakdown of these funds into various asset categories

We discussed the calculation of these numbers in the early chapters of this book. Now, based on this information, we may need to adjust our goals to make them more realistic.

## Step 6: Analyze the context in which your goals are to be achieved

Before we can properly determine the best actions to take in order to achieve our goals, we need to be more aware of all the existing internal and external factors that will assist or impede our progress toward our goals. Thus, we will next conduct a SWOT (Strengths, Weaknesses, Opportunities, and Threats) analysis to help us pick the most effective actions.

### Internal considerations: our strengths and weaknesses

These are factors that originate from within the financial planning business, and would include both our financial and personal considerations. We will want to build on our strengths and overcome key weaknesses. Examples might fall into these areas:

- Investment assets (e.g., current stocks and bonds);
- Non-investment assets (e.g., houses);
- Ratio of our expenses to investment assets;
- Risk tolerance versus required return on investments;
- Interest in working during retirement;
- Current personal health;
- Family health history; and
- Resources that could help us with planning and follow-up.

## External considerations: opportunities and threats

These are factors that originate from outside the business. They include both the opportunities we have to accelerate progress toward our goals, and the threats that could derail our progress. Examples might be:

- Extreme changes in the economy;
- Encouragement or opposition from others;
- Situational changes that would add or reduce financial resources, including financial support given to family members; and
- Getting good advice or planning recommendations from a CFP® professional (opportunity); or getting bad advice from an unethical financial advisor (threat).

Becoming more aware of certain threats – like opposition from your spouse or other loved ones to a particular financial decision – can actually be a good thing. We will be motivated to better understand the underlying cause of the opposition, to deal with it, and then come up with a better plan that will earn the full support of those around you. We also will be encouraged to make our planning efforts more collaborative than one-sided, thus getting better buy-in from key individuals.

Based on this SWOT analysis, we may adjust our goals to make them more appropriate for our situation, either raising or lowering the targets.

# Step 7: Formulate strategies

After completing our SWOT business analysis, and confirming our goals, we move toward taking actions. We will first consider the broader strategies in this step, then look at the more narrowly focused tactics in the following step.

Some of our strategies will be based on non-financial values and goals, such as improving our physical fitness. The formation of these actions are outside of the scope of this book; however, they may impact your budget and thus should be considered as part of your total planning effort.

*Financial* goals for any business must cover two areas:

## Ensuring sufficient cash flow

Cash flow is often referred to as the lifeblood of a business. Without sufficient cash, bills and employees cannot be paid, and the business may go bankrupt. Even a business that has a good accounting profit can go out of business if invoices are not paid by the customers, or if the market for its most valuable assets suddenly collapses.

Cash flow is especially important for a *small business*, which is an appropriate classification for your financial planning endeavor. A small business, unlike its larger cousins, may not easily get large emergency loans to cover unexpected expenses. It must find ways to ensure there will be adequate cash flow throughout future time periods.

In a similar same way, *My Financial Plan* – your "business" in our analogy – needs to make sure that there is sufficient cash flow available to take care of both regular and unexpected expenses.

## Achieving adequate return on investments

A business owner must generate sufficient net returns, or profits, in order to properly repay those who are financing the business. Shareholders of the business might be willing to give management a "pass" on getting high returns if the money is needed to build the business, or to weather a difficult economic period. Barring these circumstances, if there is an insufficient return, holders of shares in the business will seek to have the business sold, so that they might be able to reinvest their money in a more profitable enterprise.

In a similar way, our financial business must provide a sufficient return on our money. There will be times to be patient with our investment returns, but there will be other times when we must be willing to make prudent changes in our investment portfolio.

Financial values and goals can be achieved by the thoughtful application of strategies discussed in this book. These strategies include:

- Determining your optimum withdrawal rate from your investments (Chapter 1);
- Establishing your guaranteed cash flow (Chapter 2);
- Using the 3-Buckets strategy for portfolio composition and management (Chapter 4);
- Using tax-advantaged accounts to improve investment growth (Chapter 9);
- Minimizing taxes on your investment returns (Chapter 11); and
- Using risk-management strategies to minimize uncontrollable risks (Chapter 13).

You may need the help of a CFP® professional in developing these strategies.

## Step 8: Implement strategies through tactical actions

Once you have identified an appropriate strategy, you next determine the specific tactical actions needed to implement that strategy. Some of these tactics have been previously spelled out, including:

- Ways to maximize your lifetime social security retirement payments (Chapter 2);
- Ways to increase the diversification of your investments (Chapter 7);
- Possible use of high dividend stocks to replace some of your low-interest bonds (Chapter 8);
- Alternative means of funding the 3 Buckets (Chapter 10); and
- Possible conversion of a standard IRA to a Roth IRA (Chapter 11).

Financial sites on the internet, or a consultation with a CFP® professional, can provide other potential tactics. It would also be a good idea to talk through your action steps with a trusted family member, friend, or professional advisor. You just might be able to improve on the proposed action, or you simply might get confirmation that your idea is sound. Either way, you will probably sleep better at night, not worrying that you may have made a poor decision.

## Step 9: Put tactical actions into a plan and review

All the strategies and actions you choose should be placed into a documented plan, listing dates and responsibility for implementation of each item. This plan becomes the basis for future evaluation and follow up activities.

### Evaluate the plan results

On at least an annual basis, you should review the results from your financial plan. You can determine:

- What went well, and should continue;
- What had a disappointing, but temporary, result; and
- What did not go well, and should be changed.

To facilitate this review, you can use an aggregating tool that allows you to combine all your accounts into one place. If you have an account with Morgan Stanley, Fidelity, or Vanguard, you can use such a tool at their web site. Another option would be to enter your information into a web site such as Personal Capital. Please see the appendix of this chapter for questions to be addressed during this review.

Once your financial data is collected, it would be a good idea to have another person (such as a CFP® professional) help you make the financial analysis, and then suggest alternatives as needed.

### Consider revisions to your goals

After completing a review of your plan, you might feel that changing circumstances should be met with a change in some of your goals (and therefore your strategies and tactics).

You normally won't change your mission statement, vision statement, and values list, so your revisions would usually begin with step 4 in this process (Use Values to Create Goals).

## Step 10: Make continuous improvements

You should have the attitude that your plan can always be improved. This attitude will accomplish at least three things for you:

1. You will not obsess over trying to get the plan perfect the first time out – and then delay its implementation. Remember not to let "the perfect become the enemy of the good".
2. You will be able to take advantage of changing circumstances – a dynamic plan has inherent advantages over an inflexible plan, especially when dealing with as many variables as are present in the financial world.
3. You will be on the outlook for new methods to improve your plan.

The next section of this book will provide detailed techniques that will help you make these continuous improvements to your plan.

## Chapter summary

This chapter has given you the tools and guidance necessary to create the building blocks of a complete financial plan. These concepts and techniques were drawn from those that are commonly used in the business world to create financial plans. The chapter has shown you how to use these building blocks not only to create your plan, but also to use them as a framework for an annual plan checkup. Finally, the chapter concludes with an appendix that will help you complete an annual plan review of your financial "business."

# Chapter Appendix: Questions to ask during your annual planning review

To ensure that your retirement plans are on track, at least once a year (perhaps around your tax filing time) ask yourself the following questions:

- Are you spending too much?
- Are your account balances where you expected them to be?
- Can you take steps now to minimize next year's tax bill?
- When did you last rebalance your investments to keep the mix close to your target?

To answer these questions:

- Total up your withdrawals from investment and savings accounts. A 4% withdrawal rate of an original retirement balance adjusted for inflation is considered the maximum most retirees should take out each year if they want their savings to last as long as they do.
- Look at where your money has gone over the past year. One tool to make this task easier is a link from your bank accounts to Mint.com, where transactions can be labeled and sorted.
- Maximize tax efficiency by making sure investments are in the right kinds of accounts. For example, municipal bonds and utility stocks can be held in a taxable account, but junk bonds and high-yielding real-estate investment trusts are best kept in a tax-sheltered account.
- Ensure your investment allocations haven't moved far away from targeted levels because of swings in the markets.
- Even if equity markets have been in a rally mode, you may want to resist the urge to substantially increase your withdrawals. By keeping withdrawals steady each year, you help the flush times offset the inevitable down years.

- If you are over age 70½, combine the process of resetting portfolio allocations with planning for the required annual minimum distributions (RMD) from individual retirement accounts. You can allocate money for the RMD and rebalance your portfolio all in one move.

# PART 3

## Detailed Techniques to Improve Your Financial Plan

The following section contains detailed discussions and examples of selected financial planning topics. In previous chapters, we put aside these details in favor of addressing the larger questions. Now we will take a deeper dive into these issues.

# Applying this book's suggestions

### How to best use the "4% rule" today (Chapter 1)

Chapter 1 stated that today's retiree could reasonably expect to withdraw 4% each year from a diversified portfolio. This withdrawal rate is based on my review of a number of studies of past and projected withdrawals, including a research update by Bill Bengen, the originator of the so-called "4% rule". His original research concluded that retirees with a diversified portfolio split between stocks and bonds could safely withdraw 4% of their initial balance at retirement, and then adjust the dollar amount for inflation each year. This level of withdrawal was expected to provide a stable, inflation-adjusted income stream that had a strong likelihood of being sustained for 30 years, based on historical returns for stocks and bonds.

More recent research on this topic has included today's higher equity valuations and lower interest rates in projections of future returns. These studies suggest that a moderately diversified portfolio still can sustain a 4% withdrawal rate over a 30-year period with an 85% success rate.

However, most of this recent research, and related published guidelines, remind us to use the 4% target not as a "rule", but as a "guideline" with certain provisos. These include:

- Guidelines are a starting point and shouldn't be taken as much more than that. You always have to consider your personal situation – goals, planning horizon, and portfolio composition.
- The original 4% "rule" assumed fixed-dollar, inflation-adjusted annual spending. If you rigidly follow such a spending strategy, you may run into a problem if you encounter a prolonged period of poor market performance, especially at the beginning of retirement. To counter this problem, you will need to be somewhat flexible in terms of your portfolio composition and your annual spending.
- Since most of the published studies use benchmark returns like the S&P 500 as a proxy for market returns, with no consideration of costs such as taxes and investment fees, you will need to minimize these costs in order have the best chance of achieving the 4% target withdrawals throughout your retirement.

All of these provisos to the 4% withdrawal rate have been incorporated into the appropriate parts of this book.

## Should you have a mortgage in retirement? (Chapter 1)

Chapter 1 discussed the importance of budgeting—with an eye toward reduction of unneeded expenses. Since a home mortgage is the largest expense for most people, should everyone seek to pay off their mortgage prior to retirement? Let's look at the pros and cons of this issue.

## First, the advantages of paying off your mortgage

In recent surveys, the number one area that frequently distinguishes happy retirees from unhappy ones is a paid-off mortgage. Clearly, there is a strong positive psychological effect in having a guaranteed place to live. Having no mortgage would also eliminate a large fixed expense and the cash flow needed to pay it. Eliminating this expense has the same effect as adding guaranteed income of an equivalent interest rate. And it allows a larger portion of investment money to be put into higher-growth investments.

## But should you never have a mortgage in retirement?

Consider the positive aspects of a mortgage from this real example:

> A couple in their mid-sixties was purchasing a second home. They had sufficient funds for their retirement expenses from their retirement savings. They also had some additional funds from two inheritances. They could have purchased the house outright with the inheritance money; or, they could have taken a 15 year, no points mortgage at a 2.8% interest rate. After the income tax deduction for the mortgage interest, their effective after-tax mortgage interest rate was 2.15%.

Instead of using the inheritance money to buy the house, the couple chose the 15-year mortgage. They kept the inheritance money in a balanced fund that had an historical after-tax return of 6% per year, including an after-tax distribution of 2.5%.

In this example, the couple had the option of acting like a profitable bank: accepting money at an effective rate of little more than 2%, and then using it to receive an expected 6% return. Does the "rule" of never having a mortgage in retirement apply here? Most of us would say "no."

Thus, I believe there is no absolute rule against retirement mortgages. While for most people, it would be a good idea not to have a mortgage on your primary residence while in retirement, you should look at all the circumstances before making retirement mortgage decisions.

As a side note, if you are going to refinance or get a new mortgage, you should do so while you are still working at your primary full time job. Loan officers always want to ensure that you have sufficient cash flow to repay the loan. Thus, just having a million dollars in Amazon stock, but no cash flow other than social security, may not qualify you for a loan.

## Detailing a budget (Chapter 1)

As discussed in Chapter 1, virtually everyone has some sort of budget for their spending, even if only based on a general sense of what is affordable. Such an informal budget may work with some people that are highly disciplined spenders. However, if you need to close a big gap between your income and your spending, you will need to come up with a better, more specific budget plan.

This better budget plan begins by tracking your expenses for three months. You'll want to determine how much you are currently spending for both basic living expenses (such as food, shelter, and medical) and discretionary expenses (like cable TV, landscaping, and vacations).

Then you can evaluate and adjust these expenditures in light of your goals and income. You can use this new budget to better guide your future spending.

### Do I really have to make up a written budget?

Many people dislike creating a written budget. They may feel that it will create an unnecessary constraint on their spending, or that they'll have to generate a great deal of useless detailed information. Let's look at each of these two concerns and find ways to deal with them.

*The constraint issue*

A budget is really a spending decision guide that helps you get the most value from your money. In other words, a budget helps you spend more money on the things that matter most. Looking at it this way, one can see the budget process as giving the freedom to spend money in areas that not only cover our basic needs, but in discretionary areas that give us the highest degree of personal satisfaction.

To help create this decision guide, we first review our personal goals and underlying values – the things that are most important to us. How important is it to leave a significant inheritance to our children? At what level should we fund our church or our personal charities? Should we put a priority on extensive foreign travel? Or perhaps a winter condo in Arizona might have more benefits than just a comfortable climate?

We also want to consider the relative importance of these values; for example, how important is it to frequently see our grandchildren, as compared to updating our kitchen? It would be helpful to think through the relative value of these items, discuss them with significant others, arrive at a final ranked list, and then use that list to help us prioritize our spending.

Armed with this information, we can better make strategic decisions, such as: Should we have one car (with less expense) or two (with more freedom and less scheduling hassle)? Or, should we maintain a second home so that we can more fully remain in our children's and grandchildren's lives?

*The devil in the details*
Now we can get into the details. A budget begins with a collection of expense categories (mortgage, utilities, food, restaurant, etc.) into which we put our spending. As a side note, be sure to include budget categories that accumulate money for items that may not occur every year (like buying a car, painting the house, or replacing the air conditioning).

Budget templates (like those at mint.com) can help you determine the proper budget categories. You can eliminate categories that make the budget process detailed and burdensome. To further simplify, look for ways to possibly combine categories. For example, if you don't go out to movies or shows frequently, perhaps you can combine them into a category with "restaurants" and call it "entertainment".

However, be careful not to over-combine budget categories. If you create a general category called "housecleaning", for example, you might not notice that your inside cleaning is $1,200 a year, while your outside work is only $300 a year. That might lead you to make a poor decision as to what to do about "housecleaning" when the time comes to evaluate your expenses. You might decide to eliminate all "housecleaning", when you should keep paying for the difficult outside work, but eliminate the easier inside work.

Once you have a good working list of budget categories, you can divide them into "Musts" (basic living expenses, like food) and "Wants" (like vacations). Within each of these divisions, you can further characterize the item as "Fixed", if the expense will likely have to remain the same over the next year (like property taxes); or "Variable", if the spending is capable of being changed during the next year (like housecleaning services).

These expense characterizations will help us make adjustments to our budget. They will also help us determine our proper investment allocation (such having as enough guaranteed income, or cash, to cover our basic living needs).

As to the nitty-gritty or the mechanics of all this work: There are many ways to handle the collection of information, the setting up of a budget, and the review and modification of the budget. A traditional way is to develop your own categories and put them on a spreadsheet to collect information and track. However, there are ways to simplify this process. One way is to purchase some budget software, especially if it can tie into your existing financial information. Alternatively, you can use some free budget worksheets at the Vanguard website; or use a free service such as mint.com. Look for worksheets that will give you the opportunity to do many "what if" scenarios without reentering data. This will encourage you to more fully use budgeting to enhance your financial decision making.

# Fixed income lifetime annuities (Chapter 2)

Chapter 2 discussed the sources of essentially guaranteed cash flow. A good option to consider is a fixed-income lifetime annuity - where you make a lump sum payment to an insurance company, and it provides you with a monthly payment for the rest of your life. The annuity investment grows tax-free, and the monthly payment is partially tax-free (you pay no tax on the part considered a return of principal).

An immediate annuity is the most common version of a fixed-income lifetime annuity. The immediate annuity begins its payout as soon as you purchase it; the deferred annuity begins its payout in the future, which in turn provides additional benefits (for example, it can also be used as longevity insurance). Here are more details about these two forms of guaranteed income.

## Immediate annuity

Because an annuity's guarantees are only as strong as the insurance company providing them, you will need to make sure that the company issuing the annuity has the financial strength to meet its future payment obligations. You can review the company's financial strength through ratings issued by A.M. Best, Fitch, Moody's and Standard & Poor's. As means of providing added safety, you may wish to spread your annuity dollars between two companies.

An immediate annuity can help minimize these key retirement risks:

- Market risk. Regardless of whether the market goes up or down, the insurance company is obligated to provide you with income payments every month.
- Longevity risk. Rather than you trying to figure out how much of your savings you can spend each year before running out of money, the insurance company assumes the responsibility for paying you as long as you live.
- Inflation risk. By including an annual increase option, you can reduce the risk that inflation will diminish your investments' purchasing power over time.

A major disadvantage of an income annuity is that you must give up control of the money that you use to purchase the annuity. However, you also don't have to manage this money to generate income, and you can secure a predictable cash flow that lasts the rest of your life.

What's more, fixed lifetime income annuities are often able to provide higher regular income payments than other products, such as bonds, CDs, or money market funds, due to the "longevity bonus" they can provide. While the payments from traditional income vehicles are limited to return of principal and interest from the investment, fixed lifetime income annuities add the ability to share in the longevity benefits of a "mortality pool." Effectively, assets from annuitants with a shorter life span remain in the mortality pool to support the payouts collected by those with a longer life span.

Put simply, the longer you live, the more money you will receive. In this sense, the annuities share a feature with traditional pensions - they need only be concerned with the <u>average</u> lifespan of the pensioners. This is in contrast with individual pension plans (such as IRAs) that must consider the <u>maximum</u> lifetime of the recipient, and thus must have greater funding than the traditional pensions or the annuities.

Annuities can come with a variety of payment options and features, including:

- Life Only. You'll receive income payments over either your lifetime alone or the joint lifetimes of you and your spouse (which would decrease the amount of the monthly payment because it would be based on two lifetimes). The "life only" option offers the highest possible income payment because no money goes to your heirs. This option typically works well for those in good health and who anticipate a long life.
- Life with a Guaranteed Period. You'll receive income payments for the rest of your life. However, if you pass away before the guarantee period ends, any remaining income payments will continue to your beneficiaries until the end of the guarantee period. Here, you get a somewhat lower payment than life only,

because the insurance company is guaranteeing to make payments for a minimum number of years.

- Life with a Cash Refund. With this option, the priority is ensuring that you never get back less in payments than your original investment. As with many income annuities, you get a lifetime income payment (but typically lower than a life-only option). If you pass away before receiving payments that total your original investment, the remaining value will be paid to your beneficiaries. This means, for example, that if you are paid only $10,000 of a $100,000 policy during your lifetime, the remaining $90,000 is paid to your heirs.

- Annual Increases. This feature provides for annual increases in the payment amount beginning on the anniversary following your initial payment. The annual increase can be based on a fixed percentage or linked to changes in the consumer price index.

You should also note that payments are partially based on the general interest rates that are in effect at the time the annuity is created. Currently, interest rates are low, so to increase your payout, you should consider creating a "ladder" of annuities spread over several years. For example, you could split your money into thirds, and create one annuity per year over the next three years.

## Deferred fixed-income annuity

Until recently, people looking for guaranteed retirement income streams typically had to wait until retirement to buy immediate single premium annuities. Now, however, a deferred fixed-income annuity (DFIA) lets you lock in a stream of guaranteed income years before your retirement begins, or lock in an even higher stream of income well into retirement.

DFIA products tend to be most beneficial for pre-retirees age 55-65, who are planning to retire in five to ten years. In addition to reducing market and longevity risk — an advantage of all fixed annuities — DFIAs have the following advantages over immediate annuities:

- **Potentially higher income.** Because you typically buy a DFIA years before you retire, the underlying investments have a longer time to grow, resulting in typically higher income.
- **Chance to vary your interest rate exposure.** With any fixed-income product, the interest rates you receive depend on the rates being paid at the time of purchase. But because you can add to your DFIA before taking payments, you have the ability to adjust your interest rate exposure over time. If rates rise and you add new money, that could boost your guaranteed income stream at retirement.
- **A more appropriate asset mix.** Locking in some guaranteed income through a DFIA may give you the confidence to maintain your asset mix through market ups and downs, allowing you to establish, and maintain, an asset allocation more consistent with your investment time horizon, risk tolerance, and financial situation.
- **A means of dialing down risk.** Pre-retirees tend to shift to more conservative investments as retirement draws closer. Establishing guaranteed income well before retirement with a deferred income annuity puts that risk-reduction process in motion automatically. You might also avoid the need to sell equities at the wrong time — into a down market — to pay your expenses, because you've already put this income resource into place.

A DFIA can also be used as a form of longevity insurance, when a retiree elects to start payments at 80 or 85. The advantage here is that the retiree receives a much greater annual payment than with a more traditional starting time, and the payments assure income at a time in which other investment resources may have been unexpectedly depleted. The DFIA can also be used to help pay for a large unexpected expense, such as a lengthy stay in a nursing home.

## The advantage in delaying social security payments (Chapter 2)

Chapter 2 mentioned that perhaps the simplest and most effective way to improve your guaranteed continuing income from social security is to delay when you start receiving retirement benefits. Some people absolutely need the social security money at 62 and thus cannot consider this strategy. Others could delay the payments, but feel they would be better off taking the money now, and investing it in the stock market.

After reading Chapter 2, you now should appreciate that social security is a form of guaranteed income needed to pay your basic living expenses. Stock markets are not a source of guaranteed income. So trading the early social security payments for a stock market investment is not a good idea for most people.

A better way to judge the value of delayed social security payments is to compare them to an immediate annuity. As discussed in Chapter 2 and in the previous discussion, an immediate annuity is a form of guaranteed income, similar to social security. But you can also effectively buy an annuity by delaying your social security payment, and it's a far better deal. Compared to a traditional immediate annuity, a couple may get up to 50% more income from delaying social security payments. And their risk-free payments automatically rise with inflation.

This strategy is especially valuable now, when interest rates are so low. Annuity providers must invest in bonds, whose returns simply cannot compete with social security deferrals.

For example, let's look at a person who would get $1,000 a month at full retirement age, which is 66 for people born 1943 to 1954, then rising to 67 for those born after 1954. A person beginning payments at 62 will collect $750 a month. However, by waiting until 70, the person would receive $1,320 per month. The money not received by using this delay effectively purchases a lifetime immediate annuity at an annual return of 6.3 %; a comparable commercial annuity today would have a return rate of 3.8%.

For couples where one partner earned a great deal, and the other earned much less, the delay in claiming can also substantially improve the survivor benefit. The lesser-earning surviving person will be eligible for the higher-earning person's enhanced benefit. The result could be a large added benefit to the survivor who lives to an advanced age.

Clearly, if your circumstances allow, delaying social security retirement payments might be one of your smartest financial moves.

## The 3-Bucket approach in action (Chapter 4)

Chapter 4 discussed the 3-Bucket model of managing our retirement money. Let's now demonstrate the actual cash flows of this 3-Bucket approach.

Let's say you are retired and expect to spend $80,000 (with $56,000 in basic living expenses) per year. Thus, you will need $80,000 from your Cash bucket each year. You will be receiving the following continuing cash flow each year:

- $30,000 - social security
- $10,000 - company pension
- $16,000 - immediate annuity

You will have a guaranteed cash flow of $56,000, matching your basic living expenses. In addition, you have $624,000 available in investment funds. How do you use your investment funds to initially fill the three buckets? And then how do the buckets get refilled?

### Filling the three buckets

As suggested in Chapter 4, we want enough money in the Cash Bucket to make sure we have cash to cover a full year. So we take $24,000 and invest it in cash-like securities, such as money-market funds or short-term bond funds. The $24,000 of these securities will complete our Cash Bucket needs for one year.

Next we will take half of the remaining funds, or $300,000, buy investment-quality bonds and put them into our Income Bucket. Let's assume that we will be able to get an inflation adjusted 3% cash return from the Income Bucket.

We then take the remaining $300,000, buy an S&P index fund, and place it in our Growth Bucket. Let's assume that we will be able to get an inflation adjusted 5% market return from the Growth Bucket.

*Now let's track the cash flow between each of these buckets at the end of a year with normal investment returns.*
(Please note a couple of things. For simplicity's sake, we will first assume that the cash transfers take place once a year – in reality, you will probably want to make transfers once a quarter. And second, we will not include inflation adjustments to these numbers, which you will most likely be doing.)

In our first year of retirement, we completely empty the Cash Bucket. For the second year of retirement, we know our bucket will be receiving a total of $56,000 in regular payments from social security, our company pension, and our immediate annuity. To complete refilling our Cash Bucket, we will transfer $24,000 from our Income Bucket.

Our Income Bucket gained $9000 in the past year, so with the $24,000 withdrawal, it will be short of its $300,000 target level by $15,000. We will make up that money by transferring $15,000 from our Growth Bucket to the Income Bucket.

Our Growth Bucket likely gained $15,000 in the past year, so even after selling $15,000 worth of stocks, we will be right back to its $300,000 target level.

*How would these transfers work if we have abnormal investment returns? Let's consider several possibilities and the actions we might take.*

- A lower return rate in the Income Bucket – boost the transfer from the stocks. This is a form of rebalancing between stocks and bonds.
- A higher return rate in the Income Bucket – cut back on the transfer from the stocks. This way you can keep more money returning 5% rather than 3%.

- A lower return in the Growth Bucket – eliminate or cut back on the transfer to the Income Bucket. You will avoid "locking in" a loss of stock value to your financial portfolio. This highlights a powerful advantage of the 3-Bucket approach: protecting you from the effects of a serious drop in the stock market.
- A higher return rate in the Growth Bucket – retain the surplus to cover lower rate years. Again, you would prefer to keep the money earning 5% rather than a lower figure.
- A lower return rate in both buckets – consider adjusting down the flow from the Income Bucket into the Cash Bucket. Rather than "locking in" market losses, it would be preferable to perhaps make up to a 2.5% reduction in your retirement budget. This would be particularly true if the lower return rates are expected to continue over the next several years.
- A higher return rates in both buckets – consider increasing the flow, up to 5%, into the Cash Bucket. This happy circumstance suggests that you have the option to spend more money, particularly if the higher rates are expected to continue.

*So what would the actual numbers in my portfolio look like during an abnormal return year?*
Let's say stocks are sold on a quarterly basis to replenish the bond fund and retain the approximate 10-year "buffer". This regular selling continues with the normal ebb and flow of the stock market, including points in which stocks may have gained or lost up to 20%. Stock market losses are usually offset by bond market gains, such that the maximum net quarterly loss would normally be 10%. On a total portfolio basis, this represents 1/10 of 1%. For a full year, the maximum loss would be 4/10 of 1%. This is hardly a disaster for the portfolio. To provide some perspective, the yearly operating expense of an actively managed mutual fund is often 1%.

Stocks are not sold in an identified bear market (beyond a 20% drop in value). This will happen, on average, once every 3 1/2 years. Once the market recovers sufficiently, in approximately one year, stock selling is resumed. When the market is completely out of the bear market, the stock selling continues until the bond fund is brought back up to the 10-year level.

Conversely, when stocks have an annual gain of over 20%, the additional gains are converted to bonds until the Income Bucket reaches an 11-year payout level. This provides an offset for the periods in which no stocks are sold, and thus will help you retain the 10-year bond buffer.

# Why it is difficult to predict your exact investment returns (Chapter 5)

Chapter 5 provided my best estimates of the investment returns we might expect over the next 25-30 years. However, in today's economic environment, with its low bond yields, it can be a major challenge to accurately predict investment returns. To expand on this point, I have summarized a research report from early 2013 that predicts future returns, then I provide the actual returns for the following years. I think you will find it to be most interesting.

## Research report and prediction

Credit Suisse released in February 2013 its Global Investment Returns Yearbook for 2013, which included a study by Elroy Dimson, Paul Marsh and Mike Staunton of the London Business School on the dynamics and implications of a low-return world.

"To maintain the real value of a perpetual endowment, the withdrawal or spending rate should not exceed the expected real return on the assets. We have estimated that over the next 20-30 years, global investors, paying low levels of withholding tax and management fees, can expect to earn an annualized real return of no more than 3 percent on an all-equity fund and 2 percent on a fund split equally between equities and government bonds," the authors write.

That rather bleak outlook was a huge contrast from the returns of last 65-70 years. Since 1950, global investors have earned more than 6 percent above inflation annually on their combined stock and bond investments. Thus, the study suggests it is unlikely we'll see those higher returns in future years.

At the heart of their outlook is low interest rates. Real interest rates -- yields minus inflation – have recently been in negative territory in some countries. That's a bad sign for bonds because not only is the value of the investment diminishing in purchasing power, there is a greater risk of market value loss. Real rates could theoretically go lower, but there is a lot more room for higher inflation, which will cut the net value of bonds.

The study estimated that real interest rates may not turn positive for six to eight years, meaning many investors are looking at negative real returns on bonds and cash over an extended period.

The authors further projected a weakened environment for stocks; according to their data, the lower interest rates are, the lower equity returns are in the five years that follow. With low rates predicted for several more years, the authors estimated equity returns to be just 3 to 3.5 percent above inflation over the next 20 to 30 years. That compares to a 6 percent-plus real return since 1950.

## Results: 2013- 2015
Remember, the study predicted an equity return of 3 to 3.5 percent above inflation.

- Thus future years were predicted to have an S&P return of 5 to 5.5%
- The actual total returns from the S&P 500 in 2013 was 32.7%
- The actual total returns from the S&P 500 in 2014 was 14.4%
- The actual total returns from the S&P 500 in 2015 was just under 2%

## My analysis
Granted, the study covered a projected 20 to 30 years, and the results covered just 3 years. But what a huge difference between the predicted and the actual rates of return! On a statistical basis, the variation from

expectations is far too great to be attributed to some systemic cause in their forecasting model.

Instead, I believe they missed the power of ultra-low interest rates to create exceptionally high equity returns in 2013 and 2014. This factor will diminish greatly as interest rates gradually rise to a more normal and sustainable level. So in my view, the authors of the study missed out on the dynamic nature of the financial markets – where a pull in one market often causes an unexpected push in another one. This is why precisely predicting a single market return over the long term is so difficult.

# Should you use a brokerage or bank for checking? (Chapter 7)

## The case for brokerage firms
Here are the advantages you may find with doing your checking at a brokerage firm:

### FDIC insurance
While it is true that bank accounts are FDIC insured up to $250,000, at some brokerage firms (for example, Fidelity) it is now possible to have over $1 million of FDIC insurance coverage in cash balances swept to multiple banks. If you wanted to do that at a bank, you'd have to set up differently titled accounts or have your funds literally placed in different banks.

### Cash management services
With the expansion of online and mobile banking, brokerage firms are now able to offer a much wider range of services. These include services and accounts that used to be available only at banks, including: direct deposit, mobile deposit, online and mobile bill payment, and check writing capabilities. The brokers also can offer debit cards linked to your brokerage account.

*Credit cards linked to investment accounts*
Some brokerage firms offer you credit cards that may directly benefit an investment account. For example, your brokerage-linked credit card might accumulate cash rewards that can be directly deposited in your IRA.

*Relief from fees*
Like other consumers, you may have gotten tired of being nickel-and-dimed with bank fees, especially on services you expect to be free. In response to this consumer aggravation, many brokerage firms will offer you cash management services with no fee. For example, brokerage firms often provide free check writing capabilities and reimbursement of ATM fees.

*Trouble-free transfers to brokerage accounts*
Some brokerage firms allow you to directly link your bank checking accounts with your investment accounts. This greatly simplifies your process of transferring money in and out of brokerage accounts.

## The case for banks
Despite the expanded offerings of brokerage firms, banks provide you some advantages that are difficult to find elsewhere. These include:

*Availability of personal lending*
If you are looking for a personal loan, you will probably need a bank. Your broker will not be able to provide a mortgage, car, or home equity loan. Instead, you will likely require the services of a traditional bank or a specialty online provider of these lending products.

*A way to establish or improve credit*
Banks can help you create a good credit record, or improve on your existing FICO score. In turn, you will have a better chance of not only qualifying for a loan, but possibly getting a lower interest rate on that loan.

*Less paperwork*
The switch from a bank to a brokerage firm can create added paperwork that you may wish to avoid.

*A sense of comfort and tradition*
You may just feel more accustomed to walking into a bank or using their online services. You also may like having all your cash in one place.

# ETFs versus mutual funds (Chapter 7)

Chapter 7 discussed two somewhat-similar vehicles that can be used to collect a diversified group of stocks or bonds: mutual funds and exchange-traded funds (ETFs). This discussion will further explain the difference between the two, and will especially highlight the advantages of ETFs.

By now, you are probably familiar with indexed mutual funds, since they frequently form the core of recommended securities for 401(k)s and IRAs. Their advantages usually include such features as broad diversification, professional management, relative low cost, and daily liquidity.

Exchange-traded funds (ETFs) increase the benefits of mutual funds in several important ways. ETFs have lower operating costs than mutual funds, provide more flexible trading, have greater transparency, and have better tax efficiency in taxable accounts. However, there are some potential drawbacks, including increased trading costs and a somewhat greater complexity. There is also the possibility of greater buying and selling spreads than with mutual funds, most especially when the ETFs are traded on a high market volatility day. While ETFs do have trading costs similar to those involved in a stock or bond trade, you can control these costs by simply limiting unnecessary trades. The somewhat greater complexity of an ETF can be resolved by learning more about them, which you can begin by reviewing the following discussion.

## Advantages of ETFs
*Trading flexibility*
Traditional mutual fund shares are traded only once per day and after the markets close. Thus, you must wait, until the end of the day, before knowing the price you might have paid for new shares or received for

sold shares. While this limited trading is fine for most long-term investors, you may require greater flexibility.

In contrast, ETFs are bought and sold throughout the trading day. Share prices will vary, primarily based on the changing value of the underlying assets. This makes it easy for you to efficiently move between asset classes, such as stocks and bonds.

Making a similar move with mutual funds is much less efficient. To begin with, there is typically a 2:00 pm Eastern Time cutoff for placing mutual fund share trades. Consequently, when you place an order, you will never know what the price will be at the end of the day. As a result, you will have to wait until the end of the day to know your proceeds from a mutual fund sale. Then, if you would like to make an exact exchange of these proceeds for another mutual fund, you will have to wait until the next trading day's close to know the price of those shares. Thus, an exchange that took three minutes with ETFs might take several days with mutual funds.

ETF orders can be placed in ways just like stock orders: market orders, limit orders and stop-limit orders. You can also purchase ETFs on margin by borrowing money from a broker. If you believe the market will soon drop, you can even do short selling with ETFs.

*Portfolio diversification and risk management*
As discussed in Chapter 7, ETFs are especially helpful in providing you access to specific sectors, styles, industries, or countries. You can even buy an ETF that invests on a continuous basis in the highest yielding currencies anywhere in the world.

From a risk management perspective, you can use an EFT to diversify an overly-concentrated position that cannot be achieved by merely selling some of that position. For example, let's say over time you have accumulated a substantial gain in some utility stocks, but if you sell the positions, you will incur a large capital gain. If you are concerned about a major market drop in that sector, you can take a short position in a utility ETF, which will effectively neutralize that concern.

*Lower costs*
As discussed in Chapter 5, typically the lower the cost of investing in a fund, the higher the expected return for that fund.

ETF operations and their resulting costs are streamlined compared to mutual funds. ETFs have lower administrative, customer service, and information-providing costs.

In addition, you may benefit from an absence of redemption fees. For example, the Vanguard REIT Index Fund Investor Shares has a redemption fee of 1 percent if held for less than one year. In contrast, the Vanguard REIT ETF is the exact same portfolio and has no redemption fee.

*Tax benefits*
You typically lower your capital gains through an ETF, and your capital gains are payable only when you sell the ETF. In contrast, the mutual fund structure usually creates more capital gains, and the fund must pass along these gains to you on an annual basis.

If you are a frequent trader of ETFs, you may pay more taxes on stock dividends. In order to get the best dividend tax treatment, you will need to hold the ETF for a minimum of 60 days. One way to avoid this problem is to consider an Exchange Traded Note, which is structured to avoid the additional dividend taxation.

## Standard IRA to Roth conversion examples (Chapters 11/12)

Chapter 12 showed that Roth accounts are so valuable that they are usually the last to be tapped in withdrawing funds for your retirement. This raises the question: Should people beyond 55 convert some or all of their IRAs into Roth accounts?

The primary benefits of the conversion are to either bring more money under the tax-sheltered umbrella or lock in your effective withdrawal tax rate on the money in the IRA. After age 70½, you also might benefit from a reduction in your IRA minimum required distribution (MRD) as your Roth withdrawals have no MRDs. In addition, while inherited Roth IRAs may have MRDs, they will provide withdrawals that are usually tax-free.

Here is the ideal conversion: You pay the IRA deferred income tax with tax-unsheltered money, thus growing the total amount of tax-sheltered money; and you lock in a lower tax rate than the rate you would pay with future IRA withdrawals.

However, before you make the conversion, you need to consider the following:

- Are there other opportunities to shelter money (such as adding to an existing IRA or Roth)?
- What is the negative effect in moving the unsheltered money (perhaps tax liability for capital gains; commissions; or loss of opportunity to take a deduction for future capital loss)?
- Are you merely exchanging one pile of sheltered money for another (when you use the money in the IRA or another IRA to pay the taxes on the conversion)?
- Will you move into another income tax bracket as you convert?
- Will you benefit from a lower minimum required distribution (MRD) from your IRAs?
- Will your heirs be significantly better off with the conversion?

For those in their 60s, there may be some times when this conversion makes sense. However, in general, the conversion is more beneficial for younger folks (in their 40s or 50s), rather than for those in their 60s and beyond.

Let's look at some examples that will help to illustrate when it might be a good idea to make a Roth conversion. In each of these examples, you are considering converting a $400,000 IRA to a Roth, are 65 years old, in the 25% income tax bracket, don't see your bracket changing for the foreseeable future, and don't have the opportunity to add new money to another existing IRA or Roth.

*Example 1*
You have just received an inheritance of $100,000. Over a period of 10 years, you calculate that you will be able make an annual conversion of $40,000 (paying the $10,000 income tax from the inheritance funds) without bumping into the next income tax bracket.

Evaluation: It would probably be a good idea to convert. Each annual conversion will result in more money being sheltered. Depending on your investment composition, you might want to place the any remaining balance of the inheritance money in a tax-free municipal bond fund.

*Example 2*
You have no significant investments outside of your two IRAs. You plan to use $100,000 from one IRA to pay off the taxes from the other $400,000 IRA, converting it over a period of 10 years to a Roth. As in example 1 above, you calculate that you will be able make an annual conversion of $40,000 (paying the $10,000 income tax from the smaller IRA without bumping into the next income tax bracket.

Evaluation: This will accomplish little, if anything. You may have some potential savings if general income tax rates go up, and your heirs may benefit, but you have not increased your total tax-free sheltered income.

*Example 3*
You have $100,000 now from a $72,000 inheritance received four years ago. You invested at that time into stocks with a 4% dividend, and have had a share price gain of 40%. Your brokerage dealer charges a 2% redemption fee. You feel the stocks are a good investment. However, you are considering selling the stocks, over a period of 10 years, to make the Roth conversion. You can make an annual conversion of $40,000 (paying the $10,000 income tax from the inheritance money) without bumping into the next income tax bracket. You are currently in the 25% tax bracket. Once the money is in the Roth, you'll buy similar stocks, and save income taxes on the dividends.

Evaluation: Upon selling $10,000 of your inheritance stocks in first year, you will incur a $200 selling commission; you will also pay approximately $420 in capital gains, for a total out-of-pocket cost of $620. Once in the Roth IRA, you will save the annual income tax on the dividends: $400 X 15%, or $60 per year. Thus, in the first year, you will have a net loss of $540. In the second year, if you get a 6% increase in stock value, your selling commission cost will be $212, the capital gains tax will be $445, and you will have an income tax savings (if dividends increase 2%) of $122. Thus, in the second year conversion, you will likely have a net loss of $535.

Given this scenario, you would clearly <u>not</u> want to make the conversion, unless some other factor such estate planning had an important bearing on this decision.

## IRA MRD withdrawal strategies (Chapter 12)

Chapter 12 discussed how minimum required distributions (MRDs) considerations play an important role in figuring out the best order of withdrawals from your IRA-type retirement funds. You will need to begin planning for these MRDs in your late 60's.

MRDs must be done every year once you attain the age of 70½. As determined by an IRS table, your first RMD will be approximately 3.5% of your IRA accounts. This percentage gradually increases with your age. If you don't take the proper MRD, the IRS can assess a 50% excise tax on the shortfall – so you definitely need to pay attention to this issue. MRDs are usually taxed as ordinary income, since most represent tax-deferred income.

It would be a good idea to carefully consider how you will use your MRD cash flow. While most people will use it for living expenses, other may wish to use it for funding inheritances or a favorite charity. Here are some optional ways you can use this cash flow:

## Cover living expenses

You can arrange to have the money automatically distributed to a cash management or taxable brokerage account. This will help assure you will meet the December 31st IRS deadline to complete your annual MRD.

## Reinvest the money

You can have the MRDs transferred to one of your nonretirement accounts, where you can invest the money, following the process suggested in this book.

## Fund an inheritance

If you choose to fund an inheritance, you may want to convert some of the IRA to a Roth IRA. The pros and cons of this topic is discussed in Chapter 12 and in the previous pages of this section.

You also might consider changing your IRA investment to interest-paying bonds and dividend-paying stocks. The income generated within the account may be enough to cover your MRDs, and thus result in retaining more of the principal to pass along to your heirs.

## Make a charitable donation

To eliminate income taxes, you can convert an IRA to a Roth, then make a charitable contribution in the same amount as the conversion. However, most of the time it is more tax-efficient to leave assets in a traditional IRA, and then bequeath them to a charity. This eliminates the income taxes in the conversion, the charity gets more money, and you exclude the bequest from your own taxable estate.

Because of the importance of making the right RMD choice, you should carefully investigate any of these options before considering using them. Clearly, to avoid making a costly mistake, this may be a decision that you should discuss with a financial planner.

# Managing tax brackets in retirement (Chapters 12/13)

Chapter 12 discusses the order in which to withdraw funds from retirement accounts. As shown in the chapter, this can be a fairly complex process, largely focused on how to minimize your taxes.

In general, you will want to keep your ordinary income, which is taxed at the highest rates, in the lowest possible tax bracket. The biggest benefit comes if you can remain in the 15% bracket.

For 2016, the 15% bracket tops out at $75,300 for joint filers and $37,650 for single filers. The next bracket is 25%, so bumping up a bracket costs you 10% more on your next taxable dollar.

What can you do if your taxable income is about to push you into a higher tax bracket? The easy answer is to substitute available income sources that are not taxed as ordinary income to help you stay within the lower income tax bracket.

Here are six nontaxable income sources to consider setting up before you retire—so you'll have tax-smart choices afterward:

### Roth distributions

Qualified Roth withdrawals are not subject to federal income tax.

### Liquidation of taxable assets at or below cost basis

Even if an asset, such as stock shares, has an overall capital gain, you may have partial purchases ("lots") that are currently below your cost. These losses can be used to offset other capital gains or can be used to generate capital losses, which can in turn be used to offset up to $3,000 a year in ordinary income.

### Tapping home equity

As discussed in Chapter 13, you may wish to consider tapping into the equity of your home via a HELOC (home equity line of credit). When you use a HELOC, payments to you are considered borrowing rather than income, so they generally are not taxable.

## Cash-value life insurance

Cash-value life insurance accumulates value during your lifetime. These policies include a cash value you can borrow against without incurring taxes. If you use this strategy, make sure that the policy does not lapse, or else you may lose the death benefit and the tax-free status of the borrowed gains.

## Health savings accounts (HSAs)

HSAs are typically offered by employers so you can cover medical expenses not paid by insurance. However, these medical expenses need not be from the current year, and the money in this account can accumulate and be withdrawn tax free for future expenses, including those in retirement. And since there are no MRDs required with this account, its tax-sheltered funds should usually be one of the very last assets tapped for expense needs.

## Annuity income

Your total "annuitized income", from annuities purchased with taxable assets, has two components: taxable income and the nontaxable return of principal. The amount of taxable income depends on your life expectancy. If you purchase an immediate income annuity at a relatively late age, the income may mostly be a nontaxable return of principal.

# PART 4

## Overview
The fourth part of this book includes:

- A listing of my own definitions or explanations of terms used in the book, such as "401(k)" or "403(b)" accounts, or "shares" of a publicly traded company
- The best ways to find a CFP® professional
- Personal finance courses available through the on-line Khan Academy

# Selected Definitions

**Asset allocation or investment mix**: different asset classes, such as stocks, bonds, real estate and guaranteed investments, that are used to help achieve particular investment objectives, such as lowered risk or higher returns.

**CD**: a certificate of deposit, at a bank or credit union, that is paid out over a fixed period.

**Bond**: a security issued by a company that provides income payments plus return of principal.

**Coupon payment**: periodic interest payment on a bond.

**Charitable giving**: a gift made to a nonprofit organization, a charity or private foundation. The gift can be in the form of cash, real estate, securities, motor vehicles, etc.

**Diversification**: a risk-reduction strategy that involves spreading assets across a mix of companies, investments, industries, geographic areas, maturities, and/or investment categories.

**Duration**: the number of years required to recover the cost of a bond, considering the present value of all coupon and principal payments received in the future.

**Estate planning**: a plan that ensures assets are managed in the event of incapacity and are distributed according to your wishes at your death. A solid estate plan may also help preserve assets by minimizing estate taxes and other expenses associated with inheritance.

**Equity:** ownership position in a company, represented in a publicly held company by shares of stock.

**FICO score**: credit reporting agency's evaluation of an individual's credit worthiness.

**Fixed-income security:** loan given to a company, government, or bank. It pays a fixed amount of interest to the investor over a specified period of time.

**401(k) or 403(b):** tax advantaged retirement account sponsored by a company or organization. The account allows for organizational contributions and job income to be deferred from current income tax, and grow tax free, until withdrawn in retirement.

**IRA:** Individual Retirement Account, established by an individual. In a fashion similar to a 401(k) account, income is deferred and grows tax-free until withdrawn in retirement.

**Hedge fund:** one that uses strategies like short selling to "hedge" exposure to the market so that it might be able to do well in either an up or down market. Hedge funds are far less regulated than mutual funds. In exchange for this, they aren't allowed to take investments from "unsophisticated" investors. Some use their investment flexibility to mitigate risk, other use it to amplify it.

**Institutional Account:** brokerage or other financial account held by an entity such as a traditional pension fund.

**Investment Grade Bond**: a security issued by a financially strong company, one that is rated higher than BB by bond rating companies. Bonds rated at BB or lower are referred to high yield, or junk bonds.

**Mutual Fund:** a collection of securities managed by a financial services company, for the mutual benefit of a group of investors.

**Maturity:** period remaining before investor will receive back the principal (or initial payment) of the security.

**Retirement:** the stage in life in which individuals have given up their primary work-generated source of income, and instead will be essentially reliant upon continuing guaranteed cash flow from social security and pension-like sources, and the cash flow from their retirement investment portfolio.

**Roth IRA:** an IRA in which income tax is paid upfront, and all account earnings grown and withdrawn tax free.

**Security:** financial instrument acquired in the purchase of an investment, such as a bond, shares of stock, or a bank CD.

**Securities and Exchange Commission (SEC):** US government agency that oversees securities transactions, activities of financial professionals and mutual fund trading, to prevent fraud and intentional deception.

**Share (of common stock):** a small piece of the ownership of a company. Shares are bought or sold at stock market exchanges, such as the New York Stock Exchange.

**Short Stock Position**: the holding of stock shares that have been borrowed from a broker. If the stock goes down in value, an investor can repay the broker with shares purchased at a lower cost, thus profiting from the stock downturn.

**Stock:** security representing ownership shares in a company.

**Tax Advantaged Retirement Account**: a retirement account, most typically a traditional 401(k) or IRA, that is composed of contributions and deferred income, in which money grows with no income tax liability until withdrawn from the account.

**Tax Free Retirement Account**: a retirement account, typically a Roth IRA, in which money grows with no income tax liability when withdrawn.

**Treasury (Bond):** fixed-income security issued by the US government.

**Trust:** a legal entity in which one person or institution (the trustee) holds the right to manage property or assets for the benefit of someone else (the trust beneficiary).

# How to find a professional advisor

## At the CFP Board Site

- Go to http://www.cfp.net
- Click on the "Find a CFP® professional" tab and search for a CFP® professional in your area

## At the Financial Planning Association (FPA) Site

- Go to www.plannersearch.org
- Click on the box "find your financial planner now"

## At the Garrett Planning Network (GPN) Site

GPN is an especially good source to help you search for planners that follow the flexible approach (discussed in Chapter 14) in developing financial plans.

- Go to www.garrettplanningnetwork.com
- Click on one of the "find advisors" boxes


# On line mini-courses at Khan Academy

These are free videos, with no ads, and are nicely done. The videos run 5 – 10 minutes. Here is where you can find them:

1. Go to the Khan Academy web site (https://www.khanacademy.org)
2. Search for courses on "Finance and Capital Markets"
3. Search for tutorials in "Investment vehicles, insurance and retirement."

**Topics include:**

www.ingramcontent.com/pod-product-compliance
Lightning Source LLC
Chambersburg PA
CBHW070246190526

45169CB00001B/315